FOUR STUDIES OF
WAR AND PEACE IN
THIS CENTURY

THE WILES LECTURES
GIVEN AT THE QUEEN'S UNIVERSITY
BELFAST, OCTOBER 1960

FOUR STUDIES OF
WAR AND PEACE
IN THIS CENTURY

BY

W. K. HANCOCK

CAMBRIDGE
AT THE UNIVERSITY PRESS
1961

PUBLISHED BY
THE SYNDICS OF THE CAMBRIDGE UNIVERSITY PRESS

Bentley House, 200 Euston Road, London N.W.1
American Branch: 32 East 57th Street, New York 22, N.Y.
West African Office: P.O. Box 33, Ibadan, Nigeria

©

CAMBRIDGE UNIVERSITY PRESS
1961

Printed in Great Britain by
Latimer, Trend & Co., Ltd., Plymouth

CONTENTS

v

PREFACE

UNDER the terms of the Wiles benefaction, an historian is invited to Belfast every year, not merely nor mainly to report upon his specialist investigations, but to reflect broadly upon the research which he has pursued in the past or sees opening up in front of him. This is a challenge, and I have accepted some big risks in trying to meet it. My lectures should be regarded as a four-pronged reconnaissance of territory which is still in large measure unknown to me. I consider it a matter of urgency that academic research should systematically explore and occupy this territory.

Distinguished academic persons are invited to Belfast to discuss and criticise each lecture within a few hours of its delivery. The lecturer and his critics are fortified for this exercise by an excellent dinner. Both from the visiting team and from my colleagues in Belfast I received, as I had hoped, some searching criticism. A sample of it (submitted retrospectively by Mr J. E. S. Fawcett, who could not be present) is printed in Appendix II.

W. K. H.

Australian National University,
Canberra
12 March 1961

CHAPTER I

WAR IN THIS CENTURY

I PROPOSE to inquire what sense there is—if any—in studying past wars. Let me begin by quoting two catch-phrases.

Preparing for the last war. This familiar gibe is aimed at the politicians and the brass hats; but it might just as well be aimed at the historians, who encourage people to peer into the past (so it is said) instead of looking forward to the future. The gibe assumes that no substantial bridge exists between past, present and future; that history never repeats itself; that human experience is discontinuous, chancy, unpredictable. And so it often is. Whoever could have predicted that Hitler would be gassed during the First World War, but not gassed badly enough to spoil his voice? Whoever could have predicted the ruin which that voice would inflict upon Germany and the whole world?

Funding experience. I have a vested interest in this second catchword, for I used it in 1941 to explain the purpose of my historical work to my masters in the British War Cabinet, and subsequently I put it into the preface to my series of war-histories. The phrase assumes that history *does* to some extent repeat itself, in that *similar* situations (not identical ones) tend to recur. It assumes that an element of continuity can be observed in human experience alongside the element of contingency. It assumes that the historian can be a forward-looking person, using his understanding of the past to identify problems which are likely to arise in the future. The problems which I know best—shipping, finance, manpower, and similar humdrum things—reveal a striking continuity of wartime experience from the eighteenth century to the mid-twentieth. My colleagues, the military historians, as I shall show in a minute, have observed a similar continuity of strategical experience stretching from the Napoleonic wars—to go no farther back—to the eve of Hiroshima.

The explosion at Hiroshima was cataclysmic. It shattered the continuity of history.

THE STRATEGY OF THE LONG HAUL

Before I start to look about for any bits and pieces of experience which may have survived Hiroshima, I must give a brief account of the strategy which Great Britain pursued in her three great wars against successively Napoleon, the Kaiser, and Hitler. It has been called 'the strategy of the long haul'.[1] Its salient features can be represented in a model or chart which summarises with remarkable fidelity the common wartime experience of William Pitt, David Lloyd George and Winston Churchill.

The chart emphasises the military inferiority of Great Britain in the opening phases of her wars. Her continental enemies would soon finish her off if only they

[1] Noble Frankland, *Britain's Changing Strategic Position* (*International Affairs*, vol. 33, no. 44).

could get to grips with her; but she lies safe behind the wooden walls, or the steel walls (it makes no matter which) of the Royal Navy. The existence of this shield governs all her strategy. It gives her the time she needs for sheer survival at the beginning and for victory at the end.

The war opens with military defeat. The British people are disappointed, puzzled, angry—and, after that, dour. A nation of military amateurs sets out to make itself professional. It settles down to the long haul. This is a three-fold effort—economic, military, political.

In these days we are so well accustomed to measuring the economic effort in terms of manpower that we may find it interesting to apply the same measurement to the effort of our ancestors in Napoleonic times. Readers of Jane Austen might imagine that the war made hardly a ripple in the quiet pond of English country-life; but British casualties in the Napoleonic wars were higher, in proportion to population, even than the terrible losses of the First World War.[1] Admittedly, they were spread over a much longer period and were due more commonly to disease than to death in action: still, they are a reminder that the fighting-services in 1811 had a million men on their books out of a total British and Irish population of eighteen millions. Deductions have to be made for troops of the East India Company, foreign sailors enlisted in the Merchant Navy and the Home Guard of those days; but on the other side it might be reasonable to make some deduction from the six million people of rebellious Ire-

[1] Major Greenwood, *British Losses of Life in the Wars of 1794–1815 and 1914–1918*, Journal of the Royal Statistical Society, 1942.

land.[1] When all these adjustments have been made we see a population only about one-half larger than that of present-day Australia supporting armed forces more than six hundred thousand strong and a munitions labour-force of over three hundred thousand.[2] Great Britain's economic effort in the Napoleonic wars, like her effort in the two German wars of this century, came close to the maximum that could be achieved within the existing framework of transport and technology.

In mobilising her economic resources for war Great Britain enjoys a big advantage over her Continental enemies. Her command of the seas enables her to exploit the international division of labour by drawing supplies from the New World. At the same time, her Navy polices the blockade which denies these supplies to enemy countries. The blockade—or economic warfare, as it is called nowadays—has been to some extent over-written and over-valued; for example, far too much was expected of it early in the last war. Its effects are in large measure indirect. It was not the blockade which drove the Germans to the verge of starvation at the end of the First World War, but their own mistake of withdrawing too much labour from agriculture. Nevertheless, the blockade did play a big part in goading the Germans into this mistake, just as it played its part a century earlier in

---

[1] No census was taken in Ireland until 1821, but official estimates were made for the years 1805 and 1813. The census of 1811 gives 640,500 men in 'the Army, Navy, etc.'.

[2] The British effort against Napoleon was estimated in terms of real resources by P. Colquhoun, *A Treatise on the Wealth, Power and Resources of the British Empire* (London, 1814), and Joseph Lowe, *The Present State of England in Regard to Agriculture, Trade and Finance* (London, 1823). Lowe calculated that one munitions worker was needed for every two men in the armed forces.

goading Napoleon into his disastrous march to Moscow.

The Navy, moreover, is a flexible instrument of raid and attack. As the national mobilisation gathers strength the enemy is kept guessing about the destination of the large forces or warships, transports and supply-ships which are assembled in British ports. This growing threat compels him to disperse his forces wastefully, just as the blockade compels him to use his economic resources wastefully. The British raids grow more frequent, they grow in strength, until they become invasions of the Peninsular War type.

While all this is happening the British are pursuing vigorous political warfare. There are various ways of describing the process and the result. In the autumn of 1940, Winston Churchill might well have adopted and adapted the words of William Pitt: 'England is saving herself by her exertions and saving the world by her example.' A cold pedant might have said that Great Britain was demonstrating once again her high alliance-potential. In the model of British strategy which we are examining, the gift of winning allies and of building coalitions is an essential feature.

The long haul of economic, military and political effort approaches its climax. The tables are turned; the initial inferiority of British power has become a crushing superiority of Allied power. The enemy at long last meets his Waterloo.

My model does not tell the story of any particular battle, campaign or war, with its fluctuations of fortune, its hopes and fears, the achievements and errors of great leaders and the fortitude of soldiers and civilians. All that

I have done is to enumerate some principles of strategy which proved their validity in the three great wars of modern times.

Alas, these principles are valid no longer. Let us recall the story of their decline and fall.

The long haul takes a long time; in the French wars it took twenty-two years, in the Kaiser's war four, in Hitler's war six. In each of these wars the command of time depended upon the command of the sea. Great Britain's enemies have always done their best to break her command of the sea—or, if they cannot break it, to elude it. In the war of 1914–18, Germany's submarines came close to breaking it; but they were beaten in the end by the Royal Navy, by the British and American shipyards, and by the convoy system resurrected from the eighteenth century—a striking illustration of the continuity of history. In Hitler's war, the German submarines were beaten once again by the same methods. This time, however, the enemy possessed a weapon which might well have proved a decisive answer to the strategy of the long haul. The naval shield cannot reach to the skies; it cannot block an attack from the air. In 1940, the *Luftwaffe* set out to destroy the R.A.F.; if it had done so, the naval shield would have been pushed back from the Channel and the North Sea, and the strategy of the long haul would have been defeated. When that attempt failed, the *Luftwaffe* tried to overwhelm by direct bombardment the growing war-industries and sprawling cities of Britain. However, the bombardment was never heavy enough to achieve its purpose. Even at the end of the war, the heaviest load of the biggest bomber was only ten tons of T.N.T.; in 1940 it was far less. Besides, the enemy was never able to press the attack home in sufficient force for a sufficient time. In 1940 his bombing fleets suffered on the average a 5 per cent loss—not a high rate, if one thinks only of a single raid, but high enough to prevent him from sending out his fleets night after night, week after week, month after month, as he would have needed to do in order to destroy British industry and British morale. The *Luftwaffe* faltered, and from that time onwards air-power swung gradually round to the support of seapower. It helped the Navy to destroy the submarines; it reinforced the blockade; it inflicted massive destruction on the industries and cities of the enemy; it opened the way for the invading armies.

And so the strategy of the long haul triumphed once again. But only by the narrowest of margins. In 1944 and 1945 two new inventions proclaimed the advent of a new strategical age. First came Hitler's V-weapons. The V1, that noisy lawnmower, proved an anticlimax; it *looked* frightening, rather like a mechanical flying dragon belching fire and smoke from its tail, but the R.A.F. fighters could overtake it and tender girls operating the complicated mechanism of the Ack-Ack guns could shoot it down. The V2 was a different proposition, a rocket that could neither be seen nor intercepted but could carry a bomb to London from launching-sites over one hundred miles away. Of course, the bombs of 1944 were not war-winners. Next year, however, witnessed the second revolutionary invention—the atom bomb. Suppose that Hitler had won the race for the atom bomb? Suppose that he had been able to put atomic warheads

7

onto his rockets before D-Day? There would never have been a D-Day. The strategy of the long haul would have been beaten at the finishing-post.

D-Day and Hiroshima seem ancient history now. The V2 and the atom bomb are pathetically old-fashioned. An up-to-date hydrogen bomb is packed with the explosive power of all the bombs dropped by all the belligerents on all the countries of the Second World War. The rockets are intercontinental. It looks as if the Great Powers will soon be able to destroy each other in a matter of minutes. The long haul, which was once the very centre of British (and of American) strategical thinking, is now dead and buried.

LITTLE WARS

The historical study of war is beginning to look like useless labour. What guidance can we find in the past when past and present are separated by such a chasm? How can we find experience when its continuity has been so terribly shattered?

Still, I promised earlier on to look about for such bits and pieces of historical continuity as might be worth salvaging. Let me look now at the 'little wars'. They still afflict humanity. They seem nowadays to be with us all the time in one place or another—in Palestine, Kenya, Malaya, Cyprus, Korea, Indo-China, Algeria, Suez, Hungary, Burma, Tibet: surely there is even more fighting now than there used to be? But why should we be surprised at that? We know that nationalism tends to explode in war, and we have seen the nationalist fever spreading from Europe into Asia, Africa, the Middle East —spreading everywhere. We know that the decay of empires tends to breed war, and we have seen in this century the overthrow or decline of many empires. We know that the rivalry of great powers tends to exacerbate the hostility of smaller powers, and we have witnessed the steady and implacable growth of this rivalry. All these causes of war are just as much with us today as they were half a century ago. In addition, there is a new cause. The balance of terror between the Great Powers may restrain them from direct attack upon each other but it does not restrain them from nibbling at each others' spheres of influence. The hydrogen bomb is too big a hammer to use for cracking the nut of local aggression—particularly when the user knows that it will crack his own nut as well. The ultimate weapon is unlikely to be used, by deliberate purpose, except in the ultimate war. Statesmen are suspected of bluffing when they utter warnings to the contrary. Bluff or the suspicion of bluff encourages the gamblers. The little fanatics and the big schemers accept the risk of starting little wars.

I ought to explain what I mean by a little war, but I shall not attempt a precise definition. Rich nations measure the size of their wars by the percentages of national income absorbed into the war-effort; but this yardstick does not suit the poor nations so well. The size of a war is a relative concept; for example, the South African War appeared big to both parties when they were fighting it, but in retrospect we see that it was a little war for the British and a big one for the Boers. I propose to limit my inquiry to wars of this type, and I shall make do with a soldier's definition which was approved by the British War Office half a century ago: 'Small war is a term used to define operations of regular armies against irregular or comparatively irregular armies.'[1]

This definition does not fit every little war equally well; for example, it does not fit some wars of civil dissension and foreign intervention, such as the Spanish and Korean wars. But it does fit very well most of the little wars which the British have fought during the last century. I have studied five of these wars—the Anglo-Boer War of 1899–1902, the Irish 'troubles' of 1920–22, the Arab rebellion of 1936, the Mau Mau rising in Kenya and the Communist resistance in Malaya. I have studied the last two chiefly from printed sources, including such down-to-earth stuff as the infantry drill-books. I have studied the first two in contemporary records. I went to Palestine for a good look at the Arab war of 1936 while it was being fought, and have studied it in print since then. My knowledge you see is a bit patchy, but it is sufficient to illustrate the striking continuity of experience which has been a feature of small wars from the beginning of the century right up to the present. The War Office book which I quoted just now may look a little out-of-date here and there—for example, armies don't have to look after camels nowadays or to bivouac in squares—but nearly all its twenty-seven chapters would still have been useful reading a few years back for British officers in Kenya or Malaya. The technological changes of the past half-century have left pretty well intact the author's

---

[1] Col. C. E. Callwell, *Small Wars; Their Principles and Practice*, 3rd edition, 1906. Published for the War Office by H.M.S.O.

principles of strategy and tactics and his expositions of
hill-warfare, jungle-warfare, communications, supply,
intelligence and similar important matters.

One gets a strong impression of continuity if one
studies the soldier's drill. A soldier undergoing training
for operations in Kenya or Malaya is expected to make
himself perfect in 'immediate action drills'. Suppose that
he is with a convoy of lorries which runs into ambush
along the road: if he is the driver he must decide in a
split second whether to drive on or to stop the truck; if he
is a passenger he must be ready on the instant to jump out,
take up position, open fire and co-ordinate all his actions
with those of his comrades in the truck and indeed the
whole convoy. Or suppose that he is on patrol in the
jungle: he will be moving quietly along the trail, using
his eyes and ears like a hunter in pursuit of shy game,
ready on the instant to help set an ambush or elude one,
and ready, if he values his life, to shoot fast and straight.
Good marksmanship is just as essential nowadays as it was
in East Africa forty years ago, or in South Africa sixty
years ago.

Intelligence is just as important now as it was then.
After studying British Intelligence papers of the Boer
War and comparing them with the notes and diaries of
General Smuts, I am satisfied that the Boers possessed one
great advantage to compensate their inferiority of numbers and equipment; Smuts always had quicker and more
accurate information about British movements than the
British had about his; that is why he was able, time and
time again, to make his hair-breadth escapes through the
converging columns, maintain his small force in being

and fight back. In the Anglo-Irish fighting of 1920–22, the British commanders declared roundly that their military predominance was completely cancelled out by the inferiority of their Military Intelligence. In 1936 the British commanders in Palestine made precisely the same complaint, as well they might, for they could hardly move a platoon without the news being carried hot foot to the Arab forces in the hills. In Malaya, during the 1950's, government forces were in a better position because the enemy did not enjoy spontaneous support among the general population; nevertheless, he had established among Chinese civilians a Communist organisation called Min Yuen, which provided the guerrilla fighters with supplies and news. It was a major object of strategy to break this organisation. As always, the needs of Intelligence explain a good deal of military impingement upon civilian life. If I may return again to the Anglo-Irish troubles, their exacerbation was due in very large measure to the struggle for military information. The whole Irish population was a source of information to Michael Collins and his staff while the British commanders were working in the dark. They did their best to build or rebuild a reliable system of Intelligence while the I.R.A. used every means to prevent them. The struggle assumed the ugly aspect of gang warfare.

This leads me to the most unpleasant feature of small wars: military action against the civilian population. Let me take the Boer War as an illustration. After the fall of Pretoria and the Battle of Diamond Hill in mid-1900 there were no more regular campaigns or battles; but the Boers fought back by guerrilla tactics. So long as they could get supplies and information from the farms scattered about the veld there seemed hardly a chance of catching them and bringing the war to an end. What were the British commanders to do? Well, they had for their guidance an established military doctrine: it is legitimate to strike at enemy sources of supply; it is legitimate if need be to drive off or kill the cattle, to destroy the growing crops, to burn the barns and even the farmhouses. All this is legitimate—but is it merciful? Is it expedient? Colonel Callwell, the authority on small wars whom I have had at my elbow, praises Hoche because he combined moderation with firmness in his pacification of La Vendée; civilian populations, according to Callwell, should not be made to suffer beyond 'a certain limit'. Unfortunately, it is not at all easy to fix this limit or to stick to it after fixing it. The diaries of Smuts paint a horrifying picture of the sufferings inflicted even upon animals by the 'legitimate' methods of war practised by the British in the Boer republics.[1] Campbell-Bannerman called them 'methods of barbarism'. Yet Lord Roberts had never intended to act like a barbarian when he gave the first orders to lay waste the farms; neither had Lord Kitchener when he carried military logic to its conclusion

[1] From the diary of General Smuts, 7 August 1901:
'Aug. 7. Last night at Zandspruit. Dams everywhere full of rotting animals; water undrinkable. Veld covered with slaughtered herds of sheep and goats, cattle and horses. The Horror passes description. But the saddest sight of all is the large numbers of little lambs, staggering from hunger and thirst around the corpses of their dead and mangled mothers. . . . Surely such outrages on man and nature must move to a certain doom. English are probably in Bulfontein, still pursuing one of my small parties in front of them.'
[On his march through the Orange Free State and into Cape Colony in August–September 1901, Smuts kept his diary on the backs of railway government forms.]

in the concentration camps. A name of evil omen! But no evil was intended; it simply happened that one thing led to another in a manner which nobody had foreseen. The farm burnings were intended to shorten the war; but Smuts believed that they prolonged it by driving desperate men back to the commandos. The concentration camps were intended to save the lives of women and children; but the death rate in the camps rose to 430 per 1,000 and the total death-roll to nearly 26,000.[1] Nobody had foreseen such a tragedy; it just happened that the British Army had received a better education in military law than in diet and sanitation.

Should soldiers be entrusted with such sweeping powers over civilian populations? This is the last problem of little wars which I shall examine—the problem of military *versus* civilian control. Here again the continuity of experience is striking. During the South African War, public opinion in Britain rebelled when it realised the tragic consequences of mismanagement in the camps. The government transferred the responsibility from Kitchener to Milner. By the end of the war the death rate was down to 20 per 1,000. Here was a lesson which left an enduring impression on British thought and feeling. To this day, the bias in Press and Parliament is in favour of civilian control.

Yet there is something to be said on the other side. The army commanders said it with emphasis during the Irish troubles of 1920–22 and again during the Arab insurrection of 1936. They argued that it was not only

---

[1] My figures are taken from G. B. Pyrah, *Imperial Policy and South Africa, 1902–1910* (Clarendon Press, 1955), Appendix II, *The Methods of Warfare.*

prudent but also humane to finish the fighting quickly: but how could they finish it quickly when they were hampered by niggling civilian control? They wanted to concentrate their forces for offensive action, to seek out the enemy and bring him to battle; but the civil government compelled them to scatter and waste their forces in support of the civil police. They did not believe that the civil police and the civil courts would ever finish the job. In urging this opinion they had the strong support of the rank and file. Consider for a moment the situation of a British soldier in Ireland in 1921. He was living all the time inside enemy lines without ever knowing who his enemy was or where he was. A group of men playing pitch and toss by the roadside was such a common sight in Ireland that an enemy patrol could easily camouflage itself in this way. Men apparently engaged in work on the land could quickly form an ambush along the hedges whenever a scout or a small boy brought news of approaching troops. A gunman who shot a British soldier in the streets could pass his gun from hand to hand to women whom the troops were not allowed to search. Under these circumstances it was a marvel that the British soldier retained his discipline; it was not the troops who broke loose in violent retaliation but the police—particularly the newly recruited men who were nicknamed 'the Black and Tans'. Surely the commander-in-chief had a strong case when he asked the government to declare a state of insurrection or to proclaim martial law and thereby place all power in the hands of the military authorities?[1]

[1] From January 1920, the theory of 'military action in support of the civil

But how did the military authorities propose to use this power when they got it? They had ready a long list of measures to tighten every strand and repair every rent in the mesh of control—registration of the civilian population, identity cards, passports, curfews, summary powers of search, summary arrest, summary trial, summary punishment, drastic restrictions on the liberty of speech and printing throughout Ireland. But what about England? What good would it do to prevent the *Irish Independent* from printing what it wanted if they could not prevent the *Manchester Guardian*? What was the use of stopping the mouths of politicians in Dublin when their mouths could not be stopped in London? Military logic, it became clear, was a threat not only to Irish but to British liberties. Parliament would not stand for that.

A constitutional State, it would seem, is far less efficient than a despotic State in suppressing national freedom. Hitler was able to suppress the Czechs and Khruschev the Hungarians in a few weeks or days, but the British proved unable in two years of effort to suppress the Irish. They ended by making a treaty with them. Generally they may be counted upon to act in a similar way—not to push

power' was applied in Ireland under the Defence of the Realm Act, and from August onwards the application of the theory became more stern under the Restoration of Order in Ireland Act. This legislation granted to the military authorities powers of summary arrest, trial, and so on, which were quite extensive, but nevertheless fell far short of the drastic powers which a declaration of martial law or of a state of insurrection would have granted them. In September 1920, the commander-in-chief made his first appeal for these powers, but the British Government instead strengthened the police by forming the Auxiliary Division of the R.I.C. (the 'Black and Tans'). In December 1920, martial law was declared for four counties only. It was later extended to some other counties; but it was never made general, and the Army believed (probably correctly) that its piecemeal application was as much a hindrance as a help.

military logic to extremes, always to be ready for a deal, to work *with* nationalism rather than against it, whenever circumstances permit. In the long run, the British method enlarges the prospects of human freedom and is also a true economy of force. In the short run, the method may be expensive. Certainly, it is unorthodox. The British may feel pretty certain that their enemies will follow a different method in dealing with them, should they ever find themselves—in this alarming new world where the relative magnitudes are changing so rapidly—on the losing side in a little war.

With this macabre speculation let us conclude our inspection of little wars. We have seen that they are just as frequent and just as important (to put it no higher) as they used to be. We have seen that they pose very much the same problems of tactics, strategy and policy as they posed half a century ago. If our conclusions are true, we seem to find ourselves face to face with a paradox: a shattering discontinuity of experience in the conduct of big wars which nobody wants to fight: a striking continuity of experience in the conduct of little wars which half the world is fighting. But is this paradox as complete as it appears to be? Let us see if we can find a link between the big wars and the little ones.

WAR ECONOMY

A little war, as our generation knows only too well, can easily grow into a big war; but this link is merely potential, occasional. What we need to look for is a constant relationship, a common factor which is with us all the time and is, so to speak, built into the structure of all wars, irrespective of their size.

We can find this common factor in the economic sphere. Little wars and big wars, wars which we grade by their weapons (thermo-nuclear, tactical-nuclear, conventional), wars which we prepare for but do not fight, wars which we fight but do not prepare for; they all have one thing in common: they all have to be paid for. I recall a quip which Bertrand Russell is said to have made at the expense of Maynard Keynes, when the latter accepted a job in the Treasury during the First World War; according to Russell it was a nasty job—'maximum slaughter at minimum expense'. I am willing to accept this *jeu d'ésprit* (although it contains a logical fallacy) as an illuminating comment on the scope of war economics. It has a timeless quality which appeals to me; it is not tied to any technology but is equally relevant for the age of stone axes and the age of Sputnik.

Adam Smith looked at the problem precisely in this way. He expounded principles of economic behaviour in war-making which have found continuous expression throughout all the discontinuities of human history. Of course, his view of history was by modern standards oversimplified and sketchy: he lacked our anthropological and archaeological sophistication and envisaged the development of human society as a succession of types and stages—the hunting stage, the pastoral stage, the agricultural stage, and so on. This historical framework, crude though we may think it, was sufficient for his purpose. He wanted to clarify a problem which has confronted every human society: how to distribute its economic resources between the competing claims of 'defence' and 'opulence', between its desire as a group for security and the desires of its members for subsistence and well-being.

Primitive societies, he thought, make their decisions below the level of conscious thought. A tribe of hunters has no need to change its way of life if it encounters a hostile tribe; all its members are ready immediately to join in the fray with such weapons as they possess. This is total war, if I may use a nasty modern phrase; but it is total war of feeble intensity, because hunting societies are small and their members cannot afford to take off much time from the absorbing tasks of keeping themselves alive. Pastoral societies, on the other hand (Adam Smith was thinking of the Tartars and other Asian nomads), are able to wage total war with fierce intensity, for they are large in numbers, well supplied with reserves of food, and able to devote their full energies to battle as they advance with their flocks and herds through enemy country. Agricultural societies—to climb still another step on Adam Smith's ladder—are compelled by their static character to wage war in a different way; even if all the men of fighting age can give most of their time to war, the women and older people must stay at home to look after the farms. The principle of the division of labour begins to operate in war as in the other pursuits of society. It operates with increasing force as agriculture becomes more developed and manufacturing grows up beside it, until at last the fighting men become a minority of the people, dependent upon other classes for their food, clothing and weapons. By this time it has become necessary for the government to intervene as paymaster both of the armed forces and of the large numbers of people in many trades who produce goods and services for their support. As Adam Smith puts it, war has become an 'expense of the sovereign'.[1]

At this point in the story the successors of Adam Smith went off at a tangent. He always thought in terms of real resources, of labour and the products of labour; the role which he assigned to money payments, whether in peace or war, was merely instrumental. His successors, however, became fascinated with the problems of war finance. Admittedly, these problems are both intricate and important. The British people owe a great deal to the long line of economists and statesmen who built up their incomparable financial tradition; it explains many of the contrasts between British and German fortunes during this century to recall that our experience of the income tax stretches back to the days of William Pitt, whereas the Germans entered the First World War without any income tax at all. Despite this, the British found themselves compelled during the First World War to take up the story again where Adam Smith had left it: to take the measure of their long haul in terms, not merely of finance, but of labour, industrial capacity, raw materials, food, shipping and similar concrete things. They discovered, too, that money payments were not by themselves effective in shifting economic resources about in the vast quantities and at the high speed which national survival demanded; they found it necessary to use the

[1] Adam Smith, *The Wealth of Nations* (ed. Edwin Cannan), book v, ch. 1, part 1.

instrument of governmental control—the command ot the sovereign supplementing, if not superseding, the 'expense of the sovereign'.

It took time to learn or to re-learn these lessons and to work them out in the complicated detail that was required; but we may now flatter ourselves, after our second experience of a big slaughter, that the principles of war economy are well understood by all the Great Powers. Leaving out the complications of overseas supply (although they are immensely important, particularly for Great Britain) I would summarise these principles as follows:

First, to increase total output to the maximum obtainable by enlarging the work force, lengthening the hours of work and drawing into production all idle resources.

Secondly, to appropriate for war use (including capital development of war industry) as large a volume as can be secured of these augmented economic resources.

Thirdly, to allocate resources within the war-zone amongst the different claimants (e.g. the Service and Supply Departments) on the principle of 'maximum slaughter at minimum expense'.

Fourthly, to allocate such resources as are left within the civilian zone in such a way as to maintain the people's health, strength and will to endure, always remembering that fair shares—even of a much diminished total—are conducive to good morale.

All this is so obvious that it seems scarcely worth arguing; but its ramifications are legion and working them out has taken nearly thirty volumes of the 'Civil' series of the United Kingdom Histories of the Second World War.

What is the use of all this work? That is the question I asked at the beginning. In moments of depression I answer: no use at all. But then I change my mind. On issues of agonising importance to the human species, the work has helped me, at any rate, to think a little straighter than I should otherwise have done.

The discontinuities of history remain embedded in continuity. Our generation has witnessed a revolution in technology and in strategy, but not in politics and economics. In the new context of the thermo-nuclear age, the principles of war economy which Adam Smith expounded still remain valid. I find myself returning even to his terminology. It seems to me more realistic to think of defence and opulence as competing claimants upon national resources than to think of war and peace as separate segments of time. Wars are not switched on and off like the electric light, but are lost and won years before the fighting breaks out (if it does break out). The Battle of Britain was fought in the autumn of 1940; but the British gave themselves the chance of winning it in the winter of 1935–6, when they took the decisions which gave them their Radar network and their squadrons of Hurricanes and Spitfires: if they had postponed those decisions until the following winter, they would almost certainly have lost the Battle of Britain four years in advance. Peace, similarly, or the pursuit of it, is a continuing activity of the human spirit. Its image is in our minds even while we are fighting; its spirit finds institutional embodiment alongside the institutions of war. Were it otherwise, we should have no hope at all of rebuilding the security of mankind, no materials at all with which to build.

Yes, we make a mistake by thinking in chronological slabs, here a slab of war, there a slab of peace, so many years of war, so many years of peace.[1] Defence and opulence, war and peace, are with us all the time as alternative ends of policy, alternative activities of government, alternative postures of society. It is a question of degree: how much of one and of the other can we afford to have, or run the risk of not having, at one time or the other? The risk varies with time, place and circumstance. Frederick the Great must have realised that Prussia could hardly hope to survive except at the price of a heavy and continuous investment in defence; but to the maritime powers, and particularly to the Americans, a greater latitude was permitted. In 1939, the Americans were allocating to defence only 1 per cent of their national income. After all, it seemed unlikely that they would ever be pressed for time, for they had no dangerous neighbours and had besides two shields for their protection—the Royal Navy and their own.

Naval shields are ineffective now[2] and the Americans suddenly find themselves living far more dangerously than Frederick's Prussians ever did. The days have gone for ever when distance and the efforts of others could buy time for them; for so far ahead as they can see, they must measure their chances of survival in hours and minutes; if they propose to invest anything at all in defence, they must invest a great deal and invest continuously. Consequently, the graph of their defence expenditure is bound increasingly to assume a different shape from the one it

[1] This crude and dangerous mistake is still made: cf. the British Defence White Paper of 1958, which pictures the world poised 'between total war and total peace'.

[2] This is not to say that all naval armaments—for example, missile-carrying submarines and anti-submarine submarines—have ceased to have importance.

used to have: no longer the steep climb from valley to peak and the steep descent from peak to valley, but the monotonous, dismal prolongation of a plateau.

COSTS OF THE COLD WAR

How high can we expect the plateau to be? That is a question which cannot be answered in advance of events; but historical study can identify some of the factors which will influence the answer. Prominent among them are these three: first, the assessment of strategical need; secondly, economic capability; thirdly, political decision.

I shall discuss these three factors in their American context, partly because America is the leading power within the Western world, partly because American academic study in the field of grand strategy has achieved an enviable standard of competence and responsibility. For the assessment of strategical need I shall take as my guide a recent book by Mr Bernard Brodie, *Strategy in the Missile Age*.[1] The main argument of the book may be summarised in the following propositions:

(1) Total war in the nuclear and missile age would be a completely different phenomenon from war as it has been known throughout the previous history of mankind. No upper limit can be set to its ruinous effects.

(2) It is wrong to assume that this appalling calamity cannot happen. We must admit it to be a possibility.

---

[1] The *RAND* Corporation and Princeton University Press, 1959. The rigorous study of strategical problems by the *RAND* Corporation and elsewhere in America (and, I may add, in my own university in Australia) appears to me an important contribution both to scientific knowledge and to human survival. I would wish only that study of comparable rigour were being made of the problems which will be discussed in the following chapters.

(3) America will not take the initiative in unleashing it.

(4) In making this decision, America has exposed herself to the risk that Russia may strike first.

(5) The Russians must therefore be made to realise that the American counter-blow will be immediate and comparably shattering. This is the policy of deterrence.

(6) Effective deterrence involves: (i) an adequate retaliatory force in constant readiness; (ii) adequate protection for this retaliatory force against sudden attack; (iii) protection for the civilian population, or part of it.

(7) The policy of deterrence will be effective only in so far as the enemy believes that it will be implemented: consequently, it is inappropriate outside the area of vital national interests.[1]

(8) It follows that a 'separate capability' must be created for resisting local and limited aggressions.

Looking quickly through this list, one sees at once that its implications for the American defence bill are substantial. It means, to begin with, that the Americans must persevere in their present attempt to match Russian capabilities in the fields of nuclear physics, rocketry and space travel. In addition, they must spend a great deal of money in fields which they have hitherto neglected. Up to the present, they have done almost nothing to protect their retaliatory force against destruction on the ground—a neglect which Mr Brodie considers foolhardy in the extreme. They have done almost nothing for civil defence; but Mr Brodie now warns them that 'hopeless exposure' to H-bomb assault might sap the will to stand firm among the civilian population. Meanwhile, they have been arming their fighting formations with 'tactical

[1] A policy of 'massive retaliation' was proclaimed by Mr Dulles on 12 January 1954, when the Americans were in exasperated reaction against the Korean War; but Mr Brodie believes that they would *not* in practice 'prefer having one big war to one or more little ones'—provided the enemy gives them the choice. (Page 248.)

nuclear weapons' on the theory that they will thereby counterbalance the numerical superiority of the Russian forces. In Mr Brodie's view, this may prove to have been a short-sighted economy, because of the difficulty of drawing a hard-and-fast line between the tactical and strategical elements of nuclear warfare and the consequent danger of an upward spiral leading to the unlimited exchange of H-bombs. Obviously, America and her allies in NATO must be prepared at need to fight with tactical nuclear weapons; but this is 'a very different thing from being prepared not to fight without them'.[1] The 'separate capability' which Mr Brodie has in mind means that the Americans must now turn back in their tracks and make separate and sufficient provision for the production of 'conventional' weapons and for the enlistment of men to use them.

What will it all cost? Here, perhaps, I should make it clear that I am not submitting recommendations. I am simply an observer, reporting on what he observes. On the assumption that Mr Brodie represents informed American opinion (and there is a great deal of evidence to suggest that he does) we may anticipate a steady rise of defence expenditure. The strategical requirements which he enumerates will be translated into a formidable shopping list. Of course, the principle of economising will operate in the processes of budget-making. Resources will prove to be scarce in comparison with all the bids

---

[1] Cf. Geoffrey Hudson, 'How Tactical are They?', *The Twentieth Century*, January 1960, p. 10. 'The objective should be to reach a position in which the West can say to Russia: "If you attack us with conventional arms, we will defend ourselves with the same; if you attack us with nuclear weapons, we will hit back with them." '

which will be made for their use. At any given time, departments will be asking for more than Congress will allow, or, perhaps, than the nation can afford. The shopping lists will be pared down. Admitting all this, it still seems reasonable to envisage American defence expenditure, for a good time ahead, as a plateau with a persistent upward tilt.

Where can we expect this upward tilt to stop? I said just now that we have to consider not only strategical need, but also economic capability and political will. In the examination of economic capability, we have a great deal of historical experience to draw upon. Let us recall, first of all, the methods which are employed for measuring it. They have an interesting history. Throughout the long period when war finance was mistaken for war economy, it was usually thought sufficient to use the measurement of budgetary expenditure. However, Great Britain possessed a tradition of statistical inquiry—political arithmetic, as it used to be called—which could be combined very profitably with the realistic economics of Adam Smith. Two men who belonged to this tradition, Sir Patrick Colquhoun and Joseph Low, set themselves the task of measuring the British war effort against Napoleon. They used two yardsticks: first, the proportion of the nation's manpower absorbed into the fighting services and into the industries supporting them; secondly, the proportion of the national income similarly absorbed.

The British government used these two yardsticks during the last war. For practical purposes it made special use of the first; indeed, its manpower budgets became the main hinge of British economic mobilisation. The

Americans, on the other hand, never got to the point of operating comprehensive manpower controls; consequently, they preferred to measure their war effort by the yardstick of national income. For the purposes of international comparison, this is the handiest yardstick and it is now generally in use.

The British war effort attained the high plateau of more than 50 per cent of the national income and continued along the plateau for a period of four years. The Americans achieved for one year a peak above the 40 per cent contour. In its volume and mass, of course, the American effort far outgrew the British; but I am concerned merely with the percentage levels and the cost of achieving them. The British war effort exceeded the limits of economic prudence and could not have been sustained indefinitely, even with American support; the American war effort did not exceed the limits of economic prudence and could have been sustained at or above the 40 per cent level for years, perhaps for decades. I have no time to explain in any detail the reasoning which supports these conclusions, but roughly it is as follows: the British, during the last war, cut their living standards, depleted their capital and were heavily dependent on overseas support; whereas the Americans were able at one and the same time to give this support to the British and their other allies, to feed their immense war machine, to raise their living standards substantially and still to increase their store of capital. In the strategy of the cold war, capital accumulation is a decisive element, for it would be suicidal to buy a fleeting superiority of power this year or next at the cost of certain inferiority ten or twenty hence.

Nowadays, we have to envisage a new long haul, very different from the one that I described at the beginning: a perpetual and relentless struggle, year in, year out, to keep level with the designated enemy, *both* in economic growth *and* in readiness for war—a war which neither side can hope to win (the word victory has long since lost such rational content as it still possessed in 1945) and which neither side wishes to fight.[1] Still, both sides feel compelled to compete with each other in preparing for it, and the force of this competition tends to drive the costs of their preparedness upwards towards the ceilings that are fixed by national economic capability. The American ceiling, judging from the historical experience that has just been discussed, would seem to be situated a good deal higher than anybody so far has dared to suggest. One-quarter of the national income? Or higher still?

But this is where politics come in. May not the competition for national security and the associated political objectives reach a point where one side or the other refuses to accept the economic cost? Of the two major competitors, we might expect the Americans to throw in their hand before the Russians. At the time of the Korean War, they were spending 14 or 15 per cent of their national income (GNP) upon defence; but in the following years their expenditure dropped to 10 per cent, considerably below the Russian figure. Mr Brodie now tells them that they can well afford to climb back to the level of the Korean years, and beyond. But he does not say how far beyond. One can understand his reluctance to investigate too closely the height of the economic ceiling. Such an

[1] Possibly the Chinese Communist leaders may think otherwise.

investigation might prejudice the extra investment in security which he believes to be urgent here and now, by arousing premature but intense resistance to the great increases of taxation which may become necessary later on.

There is another political constraint upon the American economic effort. Much as they would dislike increased taxation, the Americans would dislike still more the subjection of industry and of consumers to direct governmental control. This, at least, is the impression which I get from my occasional reading.[1] Under the Soviet system, on the other hand, governmental control of investment and of consumption is used as a matter of course and with great effect to induce a high rate both of industrial growth and of defence expenditure. If the Americans remain in competition with the Russians for national security and world leadership, may not they find themselves compelled to imitate Russian methods? Even to frame such a question would seem to most Americans dreadfully un-American. For who would wish to bring the American way of life into conformity with its declared enemy, the Soviet way of life? But we are not discussing anybody's wishes. We are discussing the logic of the competition for power between two great industrial states. If their struggle for power makes them

---

[1] See, e.g., J. K. Galbraith, *The Disequilibrium System* (American Economic Review, vol. 37, no. 3, pp. 287–302) and L. Tarshis, *Alternative Control Policies* in *Mobilising Economic Resources for War*, by T. Scitovsky, E. Shaw and L. Tarshis (New York, 1951). Professor Galbraith tries to work out a 'pay as you go' system which would make it possible to combine a great defence economic effort with business as usual; Professor Tarshis believes that the system, with its expenditure rationing and crushing burden of taxation, would still need to be shored up by a considerable extension of governmental control.

progressively akin to each other in their institutions and values, this need cause no surprise to the reflective historian, who knows only too well the tendency of deep-seated antagonisms to produce a measure of similarity in the antagonists.[1]

I shall now pursue logic into the realm of fantasy. Mr Brodie, you will remember, includes civil defence in his strategical agenda. He thus raises a very different subject. There are many good reasons, psychological and political as well as economic, why neither the Russians nor the Americans should wish at present to invest too heavily in civil defence. Still, the Swedes are reported already to have invested in it very heavily, and a beginning has been made both in the Soviet Union and the United States. We shall have no reason to feel surprised if the competition for power forces this investment upwards. Mr Brodie believes that 'hopeless exposure' to the threat of thermo-nuclear bombardment might sap the nerves and will of the American people, and he argues that quite a lot of protection might be provided for them at a comparatively low cost. Quite a lot? Well—he says in effect—provision might be made for saving half the American population or even more. . . . But might not the other eighty million or so people, who would still remain in 'hopeless exposure' to the threat of H-bombs, argue that it would be sound economy to make similar provision for saving *their* lives, even at the cost of additional taxation and governmental regimentation? But now we are approaching the realm of the fantastical. I

[1] Cf. Charles de Visscher, *Theory and Reality in Public International Law* (trans. P. E. Corbett), Princeton, 1957, pp. 82–4.

find myself calling to mind E. M. Forster's story, *The Machine Stops*. It opens with the whole of humanity living underground. And why not? Our scientists and engineers, who are following the writers of fiction into outer space, should find no greater difficulty in following them into the bowels of the earth. Surely the Americans could spare enough from their national income to make Mr Forster's imaginary world the real world of A.D. 2000 or thereabouts? And may I just slip in a modest proposal of my own? Botanists are experimenting with a machine called the phytotron. Let us make full use of this excellent machine in our operation Mendip. Let us take it with us when we go underground. We shall then be able to count with confidence on ample supplies of nutritious and palatable duckweed.

On the assumption (which of course can be questioned) that the Cold War continues, all this seems to me to be implicit in its logic. Still, I call to mind some reflections in the first chapter of *Vom Krieg*, the masterpiece written a century ago by the greatest modern student of strategy, Karl von Clausewitz. After demonstrating to his own satisfaction that there exists no theoretical limit to the use of force, Clausewitz wrote this sentence: 'The probabilities of real life take the place of the extreme and absolute demanded by theory.'

CHAPTER II

FROM WAR TO PEACE

IN my attempt to elucidate the business of making war
I employed the method of the social scientist, who
examines the phenomena of human societies as it were
from the outside, groups like with like in the light of such
theory as he has in his head and endeavours to discover
patterns and regularities, if not laws. This is a method
which I should not dare to employ in probing the far
more various and variable problems of making peace.
Today I shall be more of a humanist. I shall try to get
inside the mind of a representative man of this century
who gave to war-making one year in four of his political
life yet considered every one of these years an interrup-
tion of his proper business, which was peace-making.

The man was Smuts. I shall try to enter his mind at
the crisis-time of two tragic peace conferences, the first
at Vereeniging in 1902, the second at Paris in 1919.[1]

AT VEREENIGING, MAY 1902

Up to the early months of 1902, the military and political
correspondence which Smuts conducted was still exub-
erant in tone and the quotations which he wrote into his
notebooks from Carlyle, Byron and other militant

---

[1] I shall not give here references to the Smuts Archive, which contains
most of the material on which this study is based. The documentation will
be given fully and precisely in work shortly to be published.

authors breathed the spirit of patriotic defiance; but by May, if not earlier, he had begun to write in a vein of stoic fortitude. He had good reason. While his own campaign in Cape Colony was still heroically ablaze and he was taking the surrender of little mining townships in the sandy wastes up north, the two Boer governments were already halfway down the slippery slope of negotiation which led them to the surrender of republican sovereignty and the affirmation of loyalty to King Edward VII. In the second week of May, when Smuts arrived in Vereeniging under a safe-conduct from Lord Kitchener, he found himself face to face with questions like these: Could the republics still fight on or were they beaten? If they were beaten, what would remain of life and hope for a republican soldier?

Let us listen to him as he gives the answers.

12 May, to his wife. (She was kept under detention by the British at Pietermaritzburg; she was ill; for a whole year not a single letter or message from her husband had come through to her.)

What the upshot of the present negotiations will be [he tells her] I cannot say. . . . Nothing will, however, deter me from doing my duty, for I do not regard the favour either of my friends or my enemies but shall ever strive to do my duty, to retain my own self-respect and sense of personal rectitude and—last not least—the goodwill and respect of her who is the last thing left me in this life. A man may lose his possessions, even his home and country, but he may yet remain a citizen of that larger and higher kingdom whose limits are conscience and the aspirations of humanity.

26 May, to his wife. (He knows by now that she is dangerously ill. He knows also that the Republicans are doomed, for he has been in debate with Kitchener and Milner and they have made it plain that they will never loosen their stranglehold on the Boers.)

As we lose in worldly possessions, in political status and in the outward accompaniments of wealth and power and influence, we shall be thrown back all the more powerfully upon ourselves and each other. Hand in hand, and soul in soul we shall go through life, and no noise of the outside world shall penetrate into our little sovereign Kingdom of the soul.

30 May, in the Assembly of the People at Vereeniging. (He is speaking towards the close of the great debate, the day before the British ultimatum is due to expire.)

Brothers, we resolved to stand to the bitter end; let us admit like men that the end has come for us—has come more bitterly than we had ever thought possible.

In a moment or two we shall try to explore what lay behind and beyond this bitterness of defeat; but first let us move forward seventeen years and listen to the same voice crying out in the bitterness of victory. Throughout the last six weeks of the Paris Peace Conference Smuts is fighting an agonising battle within his own mind: will he or will he not sign a Treaty which he believes to be unjust and ruinous?

AT PARIS, MAY AND JUNE 1919

20 May, to his wife.

It is a terrible document, not a peace treaty but a war treaty, and I am troubled in my conscience about putting my name to such a document. . . . My children must never be ashamed of their father's signature. Is that not so, Mamma? . . . If the Germans refuse to sign, I shall very probably set a campaign going in the press and on the platform. . . . If necessary, I shall resign as Union minister and sell *Goedgevonden*[1] to get money to keep us going in the meantime. I hope all that will not be necessary. But, Mamma, you have the right to know all my plans and thoughts. So I write in good time. . . .

30 May, to Miss Alice Clark.[2] (The Germans have just submitted their observations on the draft Treaty.)

They raise the point to the very forefront which I have always considered vital, viz. that we are bound by the correspondence of last October and November to make a Wilson peace—that is, one within the 4 corners of the Wilson Points and Speeches. This was a solemn international engagement which we must keep. It would be dreadful if, while the war began with a 'scrap of paper', it were also to end with another 'scrap of paper' and the Allies' breach of their own undertaking. I am going to fight it out on this basis.

2 June, to Lloyd George.

I wish to make it quite clear that I cannot agree to anything less than I proposed at the beginning of the meeting,[3] viz. the Peace Treaty should be recast and transformed, so as to be more in accord with our solemn undertakings, our public declarations, and the requirements of a reasonable and practical policy. . . . [Smuts gives a list of the drastic alterations which he deems essential.] This programme I must now stand by.

3 June, to Mrs Gillett.

I am not budging an inch. . . . But I have little hope. The last battle of the war is being fought out in Paris, and we look like losing that battle and with it the whole war.

---

[1] One of his farms, usually called *Welgevonden*.

[2] Miss Clark and Mrs Gillett (*née* Margaret Clark) were sisters of Quaker descent and upbringing. Smuts was very much at home with the whole clan of Clarks (of Street in Somerset).

[3] The historic meeting of the enlarged British Delegation at Paris, 30 May–1 June.

4 June, to Lloyd George.

Perhaps the main difference between us is that you are in the water, while I shout advice from the shore.

10 June, to his wife.

I continue to feel very bad about the way things have gone and doubt whether I shall be able to sign this peace. . . . Sometimes I feel as if this death sentence upon Europe must be torn to pieces and as if I must set the work going before I return to my dear ones. And then again I feel what is the use of all this toil? It will and must all soon collapse anyway. Leave this Treaty to its own devices, and it will soon come to an end. So my mind swings from one side to another.

21 June, to General Botha.

In any case, my mind is fully made up not to sign.

23 June, to Mrs Gillett.

I am not going to sign it on any account.

24 June, to Mrs Gillett.

After all, I am going to sign the Treaty.

25 June, to Miss Clark.

It has been an awful thing making up my mind to sign the Peace Treaty with which I so thoroughly disagree. But I have gone through the war of which this is merely the end, perhaps the inevitable end; and I feel I am no better than the others, and that I must stand in the dock beside them. And God be merciful to us poor sinners.

25 June, to Mrs Gillett.

Yes, I have gone and done it.

We shall see later on what made him do it and we may

thus learn something about the dangers and difficulties of peace-making on the grand scale. But now we must turn back to the small-scale peace-making of Vereeniging.

The idea has got into the heads of many British people (if there were time, I might suggest how it has happened) that the Peace of Vereeniging was a magnanimous settlement. It was the very opposite. Admittedly, it contained more provision for financial aid to the shattered Boers than had been visible in the peace proposals made the previous year at Middelburg. Admittedly, it showed less concern for the rights of non-Europeans than had been expressed hitherto in British official statements: Lord Milner and his political masters in London had made a great song before the war about the denial of rights by Paul Kruger's government to Indians and coloured people; but they now treated these rights as expendable: moreover, they accepted an amendment to their original proposals which had the effect of leaving it to the Boers to decide later on whether or not Africans in the old republics would ever be granted political rights. Thus far they went in deferring to Boer interests or sentiments. But on the issues which they thought important—those that affected British political and cultural supremacy over the Boers—they conceded nothing at all.

The Boers, on their side, had brought themselves to conceding a great deal. On 11 April, when Smuts was still winning his spirited little victories in far-away Cape Colony, the two republican governments had agreed upon peace proposals which were prefaced by an explicit repudiation of the British annexations; but next day, when they met Kitchener, they allowed him to cut this preface out before telegraphing their proposals to London. On 14 April, when Kitchener and Milner communicated to them the uncompromising answer from London, they asked for a statement of the terms which His Majesty's government would grant 'subsequent to a relinquishment of Independence'. This request, one might have thought, brought them almost to the bottom of the slippery slope; but they could say that they were making it merely for information, since their independence could not be given up except by vote of an Assembly of the People.

The proposals which emerged from the first session of this Assembly (15–17 May) were as follows:

(a) Surrender of all foreign relations and embassies;
(b) Acceptance of the protectorate of Great Britain;
(c) Surrender of portions of the territory of the South African Republic (i.e. the goldfields and Swaziland);
(d) Conclusion of a defensive treaty with reference to South Africa.

All this, one would have thought, was a sufficient basis for British supremacy in South Africa. But supremacy was not enough for Milner; British domination was his aim. He achieved it—but for how long?—towards midnight on 31 May, in a document which stipulated, among other things, immediate and complete surrender by the Boers, recognition of King Edward VII as their lawful sovereign, recognition of English as the official language of their country and as predominant in their schools, acceptance in the here and now of alien, autocratic rule. To be sure, the prospect was held out to them of evolution by stages towards self-government. Jam tomorrow! There was nothing in the Treaty to tell the Boers when this tomorrow would arrive. Milner, we know, did not intend it to arrive until white South Africa had become predominantly English-speaking. That would have meant never.[1]

Of the sixty Boers assembled for debate at Vereeniging, all but six—three Transvaalers and three Free Staters—gave their votes for accepting this bitter and brutal treaty. Why? The agonising decision which they had to make was put to them squarely by Smuts: 'Hitherto we have not continued the struggle aimlessly. We did not fight merely to be shot. We commenced the struggle, and continued it to this moment, because we wished to maintain our independence, and were prepared to sacrifice everything for it. But we may not sacrifice the Afrikaner people for that independence.' Here was the crux. The British stranglehold could not be broken. The independence could not be saved, even if the Boer remnant fought on. But the people could still be saved.

Saved for what destiny? To fight another war and take their revenge upon the British when the opportunity offered? Some of the Boers had this idea in their heads, not only in 1902 but in 1914 and in 1939. Smuts recognised the power of this idea, but his own idea was different and, so he believed, more powerful. As the war was drawing to its close he had written down the two alternatives which he saw in the future: South Africa could become either a second Canada or a second Ire-

[1] Milner is supposed to have been good at figures; but demographic figuring, which was of vital consequence for his policy, seemingly had no interest for him.

40

land. He passionately desired the first alternative; but
that, he said, depended upon the British. Four years later,
he said the same thing to Campbell-Bannerman. 'Do
you want friends or enemies? You can have the Boers as
friends, and they have proved what quality their friendship may mean. I pledge the friendship of my colleagues
and myself if you wish it. You can choose to make them
enemies, and possibly have another Ireland on your
hands.' But that would mean civil war in South Africa.
Surely there had been enough of that? Smuts wanted
desperately to get the two white peoples out of the chasm
which had engulfed them. He told his comrades at
Vereeniging that they had fought their war of freedom
'not only for the Boers, but for the entire people of South
Africa'. In preparing his mind for the great debate he
had written into his notebook Abraham Lincoln's words
about binding up the wounds of war. Those words were
still ringing in his head when he wrote to his wife, the
day after the Treaty was signed: 'Let us do our best to
bind up the old wounds, to forgive and forget, and to
make the future happier than the past has been.' It was
in the same spirit, three years later, that he wrote his
letter of farewell to Lord Milner, the man he had always
looked upon as the arch-enemy of his people. 'History,'
he declared, 'writes the word "Reconciliation" over all
her quarrels.' What magnanimity! But Milner returned
him a cold answer. Smuts did not find the response that
he was looking for until 7 February 1906, when he talked
face to face with Campbell-Bannerman. So far as he was
concerned, peace was made that evening between Briton
and Boer.

Let us pause to consider some of the features of that peace.

First, it was simple: a straight two-party agreement between Britons and Boers—or, if one thinks of the political entities, between Britain and the emergent South Africa.

Secondly, it took a long time to make and work out: the historic encounter between Smuts and Campbell-Bannerman marks the halfway stage between the Treaty of Vereeniging in 1902 and the inauguration of the Union in 1910.

Thirdly, it was contagious. 'The contagion of magnanimity'— Smuts coined that phrase forty years later in a tribute which he paid to the memory of Campbell-Bannerman. He was thinking, among other things, of the Commonwealth, as he and Merriman had prophesied its advent in Lord Milner's day, as he had proclaimed it in name and substance during the first World War, as he had striven for it in the great crises of South African, Irish and Indian history. In 1906 he had called Campbell-Bannerman 'the rock'; he felt in his old age that all his work for the Commonwealth was built upon that rock.

But fourthly, it was incomplete. Smuts liked to think of the contagion of magnanimity spreading downwards from the leaders to the peoples, but all the time a different contagion was spreading among his own people. Predikants, politicians and school teachers taught the rising generation never, never to 'forgive and forget'.

There was, besides, another and still more damaging element of incompleteness in the peace that was made between Boer and Briton. In every two-party agreement it is prudent to inquire whether there is a third party which should be represented: or, if not represented, consulted: or, if not consulted, at least remembered. In the agreement between Boer and Briton, the unrepresented, unconsulted, unremembered third party was the non-European population of South Africa.

Among the few people who realised, at that time, the

full significance of this fatal flaw was Smuts's best friend
at Cambridge, a crusty but wise old don who told him,
while he was still riding the crest of his optimistic wave:

The native question is, I know, a thorny one, but I cannot help
regretting that you do not see your way to the cautious and gradual
granting of the franchise to such of the natives who by education,
etc., show themselves capable of exercising it. No class of subjects
with any degree of intelligence and ambition to raise its standard of
living and enjoy its rightful share in civilisation has ever obtained
justice from a ruling class, over whom they have no control or
check by a share in the representation; and no such class will ever
be content to remain in such subjection.

These trenchant sentences open up a theme too large and
complicated to be pursued within the framework of this
lecture. We must stick to the agenda paper now in front
of us and follow Smuts from Vereeniging to Paris.

We have already looked into his mind as he swung this
way and that in May and June 1919. To sign or not to
sign: that was the question. It was a question deeply
rooted in everything that he had thought and done not
merely since his arrival in Paris the previous January but
since his arrival in London nearly two years earlier. The
starting-point of his thought—in all the wars that he
fought, not only the war of 1914–18—was the primacy
of politics over strategy, of peace-aims over war-
measures: let governments first make clear to themselves
what kind of peace they really need, and they will find
themselves more than halfway to knowing what kind of
war they must prepare for and fight—if indeed they find
it necessary to fight at all. Here I must cast back for a
moment to his South African experience: he never ceased

to believe that the Anglo-Boer war, like its precursor, the Jameson Raid, was from the British point of view an unnecessary and costly blunder: that the British could have safeguarded their essential interests in South Africa without fighting. And even after the war had started (I am now saying what I *think* he believed, although I cannot prove it) there was no real need for the British to fight to the finish at Vereeniging: they could have secured a just and durable peace a year earlier, if only they had pursued their real interests instead of their passions and their pride of power.[1] If Smuts was right in holding these opinions, how much suffering, how much hatred might have been spared South Africa. How much happier his country might be today.

Whether he was right or wrong about the Anglo-Boer war, Smuts wanted the British to fight their first war against Germany for precise and limited objectives, based upon a realistic stock-taking of essential British interests. He wanted, if he could, to spare Europe—'poor old Europe, the mother of civilisation, the glory of the human race'—those extra months or years of unnecessary agony which he knew by experience to be so ruinous.

Not that he believed that the war of 1914 could have been avoided by the British, any more than the war of 1899 could have been avoided by the Boers. In 1899 he had striven for peace until he saw disappear the last chance

---

[1] The assumption underlying this sentence is that the British could have had peace at Middelburg in 1901 if they had been content with a limited victory and limited objectives; but the assumption cannot in fact be tested, since the British (and particularly Milner) were out for total victory. It should however be recorded that Kitchener told Botha in June 1911 that 'if England had listened to me at the Middelburg negotiations' she would have saved herself '£100,000,000 and thousands of lives'. (Botha to Smuts, 15 June 1911.)

of securing it by a reasonable compromise, and he had exclaimed, even while the commandos were clattering past his window on their way to the Natal frontier: 'If there were only another John Bright!' But the John Brights of this world were out of favour in the England of Joseph Chamberlain. Still more were they out of favour in the Germany of the Schlieffen Plan. A telegraphic summary of what Smuts felt and thought in the war of 1914–18 would run something like this: Fight we must. Victory we must have. But not the knock-out blow. Limited objectives. 'I want no overwhelming victory.'

These five last words are his own. They were wrung from him in the agonising struggle of the spring of 1918. Yet in substance they were no different from what he had been saying, in one way or another, ever since his arrival in England, and what he would keep on saying right up to the end of the war—saying always the same thing in his letters, his memoranda, his speeches. He said it, for example, in a speech that he made in Glasgow on 15 May 1918—a speech so shattering in its forthrightness that most of the newspapers kept quiet about it. He had two themes to expound, which superficially seemed to be in violent contradiction with each other: we must steel our wills for a long war; we must prepare our minds for an early peace. The war would indeed be long if the Germans were to break through in the west as they had broken through in the east! In a lurid flash of his imagination, Smuts saw the war-map of 1940 unrolling in front of him. The spectre intimidated him no more than it did Churchill twenty-two years later. Britain would defy the tyrant; she commanded the oceans and would lead the continents into battle; she would plan and deliver the victorious counterstroke, no matter how long it took her. 'If necessary for years. . . .' Smuts was inviting his audience to face, and not to fear, the worst that might happen. But he did not expect it to happen. He had many good reasons for believing that the enemy would fail—was failing already—to win the battle in France. But that would mean they had lost the war! Smuts by now was well launched upon his second theme: the Germans were fighting an offensive war for unlimited objectives, the Allies a defensive war for limited objectives; the Germans must march to Paris, the Allies need not march to Berlin. Soon, very soon, the Germans must realise that Paris and victory were beyond their reach. The time would then come—perhaps it had already come —for informal soundings to find out whether they were ready to make peace, not on their terms, but on our terms.

Smuts had in his head, and set down many times on paper, a clear statement of these terms, in principle and to some extent in detail. He identified three main objectives of British policy:

First, security of the sea- and air-communications of the Commonwealth. This, in his opinion, meant dispossessing Germany of all her colonies and securing a strategical hold over large ex-Turkish territories.

Secondly, stability in continental Europe. This meant a restraint both upon the claims of France (for herself and for her eastern clients) and upon the expansionist urge of Russian Bolshevism. It meant maintaining Germany as a strong State within the Allied orbit. Smuts would also have wished, if it had remained feasible, to maintain the unity of the Danubian area through a creative transformation of the Hapsburg Empire into a Commonwealth on the British pattern.

Thirdly, establishment of new institutions for the maintenance of international order and freedom. His ideas under this head found expression in December 1918, in his famous treatise on the League of Nations.

These three objectives represented something more than a realistic calculation of interests; they were just as much the expression of aspirations. Mingled within them were different impulses and aims which were likely to call forth contrary responses from different types of people. For example, Smuts's friend Amery, that serene realist, approved the first objective but thought the third moonshine. His Quaker friends, on the other hand, applauded the third, but had doubts about the first. The second objective was acceptable both to Amery and the Quakers, for it represented a blending of the realism and the idealism which were equally native to Smuts. A Carthaginian Peace (the phrase was to be his gift to Keynes) seemed to him both imprudent and wicked. His encounter with Campbell-Bannerman twelve years earlier had confirmed him for ever in the belief that magnanimity was a shining virtue both in the political and in the moral life of mankind.

However, in the summer of 1918 it was not what Smuts and his friends thought about the principles of peace, but what the Germans thought about them, that mattered most. And here Smuts might well have taken warning against excessive optimism from his own exposition of German war-aims. If the Germans really were fighting an offensive war for unlimited objectives, was it likely that they would admit all of a sudden the limited defeat which was the other side of the medal to his own programme of limited victory? Botha might have been ready for this in March 1901; but Ludendorff was not ready for it in August 1918. Indeed, the alternatives of total victory or total collapse were built into the very structure—even into the financial structure—of the German Empire. And so the German High Command missed the chance, while there was still time, of shortening their lines of communication and their fighting fronts. They held on in advanced positions until the soft underbelly of their military power was pierced and its hard carapace cracked.[1]

Smuts had been slower than Lloyd George and some other politicians (but not slower than the military experts) to recognise the swift advent of victory. All the same, he struggled to the very end for a victory which would fall short of being 'overwhelming'. And here I feel constrained to pause for some further reflection upon an attitude so unusual. After all, Smuts had been as ardent in the fight as any of them. He had fought in South-West Africa and in East Africa. He would have fought in Palestine if he had been able to get 'the tools for the job'. He had offered to lead the Americans into battle. He had established the Royal Air Force. He had controlled the pattern of British war-production. No man had packed a bigger punch than he. And yet he wanted to pull his punch just as it was smashing home! He made this attempt by raising a point of procedure. He wanted

---

[1] In all this they went counter to the opinion of Schlieffen, the author of the invasion plan in the West. He had declared that, should the initial onslaught fail to achieve a decision, Germany should take immediate steps for a negotiated peace.

to see Preliminaries of Peace agreed and signed with the enemy in advance of the Armistice. Under this procedure, there would have remained a good deal to be worked out later on at the Peace Conference; but the broad lines of the peace would have been firmly drawn while the Germans still had their main forces armed and in the field.

This prospect was unattractive both to President Wilson and to Marshal Foch. Wilson was bent first and foremost upon securing public and universal acceptance for his Points, Principles and Particulars (twenty-three of them in all). In this aim he succeeded, subject to two Allied reservations which were communicated to and accepted by the Germans, and one American 'Interpretation', which was thought not to be their concern.[1] Foch, meanwhile, was intent upon securing for his side a monopoly of military power. He, too, succeeded, even more completely than Wilson did.

Smuts was afraid that the monopoly of power would play a larger part than the Presidential speeches in shaping the peace settlement. Still, his hopes were in the ascendant over his forebodings when he went to Paris in January 1919. He had just produced his treatise on the League and still felt the exhilaration of that creative effort. He knew that Wilson was reading the treatise and soon found out that he was appropriating most of its argument. This was splendid, for Wilson was the Chairman of the Commission on the League; he was driving hard to get the Covenant drafted with all possible despatch; he was determined to have it included in the Treaty. For the

---

[1] In expounding this Interpretation, of which he was the author, Colonel House told the Allies that they would be able, under President Wilson's speeches, to establish 'any point you wanted against Germany'.

first three or four weeks of the Peace Conference, Smuts felt that he had good reason for hoping that 'the things that matter' would go well.

It was towards the end of March that his forebodings began to predominate over his hopes. At that time he was in London on South African business and cooped up in the Savoy after a severe attack of influenza. He found himself suddenly afraid that things were going dangerously wrong and upon his return to Paris found his fears confirmed. These days mark the beginning of the long series of memoranda and letters with which he kept bombarding Lloyd George—and Wilson too, now and then—from late March almost to the end of the Peace Conference. Throughout the same period he was expressing his apprehension and anger in letters to his friends almost every day; in times of crisis he might write two or three long letters on the same day. It is from this vivid and voluminous material that I shall distil his misgivings about the Treaty as it took shape.

His arguments fell into two categories, the prudential and the moralistic. His prudential reasoning was founded upon the traditional British concept of a 'just equilibrium'. He felt that he was witnessing a reckless and calamitous destruction of the balance of power. In his diagnosis he started with Bolshevist Russia and worked from there westwards. He was not an interventionist; on the contrary, he pleaded for 'a Gallic-like impartiality' in the domestic struggles of Russia. 'Leave Russia alone, remove the blockade. . . . If we have to appear on Russian soil at all, let it be as impartial, benevolent friends and helpers, and not as military or political partisans.' All the same, he recognised the explosive, expansionist force of Bolshevist Russia and asked what kind of barrier the Paris peacemakers were building to contain it? Military defences, he believed, were essential, for the Bolshevists would use military force if they were given the chance. Moral defences were equally essential, for they were already using the weapon of propaganda. Against this weapon, the only defence was confidence among the Western peoples that their order of civilisation was worth defending.

From both these points of view, Smuts saw nothing to reassure him in the emergent configuration of Europe. Along the western borders of Russia a chain of new states or would-be states stretched from the northern to the southern sea—each state too weak to defend itself and all of them too greedy and quarrelsome to pool their defences. A flimsy line of outposts! What lay behind this line? The Hapsburg Empire, which for all its faults had been a solid counterpoise to Russian power, no longer existed. The only remaining counterpoise was Germany. To Smuts it seemed self-evident that a strong and stable Germany was essential for a strong and stable Europe.

He did not think it possible to destroy Germany. Sooner or later, she was bound to resume her place as the dominant factor in Europe. But that was taking the long view. In short term, the Allies could certainly succeed in making Germany powerless. But at what a price! Was it their purpose to leave the whole of eastern and central Europe open to the Bolshevist flood? Or did they have it in mind to provoke a German combination with Russia?

I have not the time to explore further this preview of the year 1939. Nor have I the time to give any further examples, no matter how severely abridged, of the case which Smuts built up against the emerging Treaty upon the grounds of *raison d'État*. From his prudential reasoning I must now turn to his moralistic reasoning. And here, just for the sake of a change, I shall begin, not with the large issue, but with 'the pinpricks', as he called them. As the draft chapters of the Treaty came in, one after the other, he found them to be infused with 'a petty, small spirit'. 'And of all shortcomings,' he exclaimed, 'this is the worst. There is something of value even in vindictiveness, but in the merely small and trivial we seem to reach an absolute zero. . . .'

Of course, what he was craving for was the positive virtue of magnanimity. In a letter to Lloyd George of 26 March, he reminded him of the part that he had played, as a member of the Liberal government of 1906, in the miracle of magnanimity wrought in South Africa by Campbell-Bannerman. In the same letter he used a synonym for magnanimity which was destined, alas, to become a sinister addition to the political vocabulary. His new word was *appeasement*. Other people used it once or twice in the correspondence of that time and Smuts himself used it in public print before he left England. But it was not until the false dawn of hope at the Locarno Conference of 1924 that the word became common currency. Throughout the Briand–Streseman era of the 1920's, *apaisement* was the symbol of reconciliation between France and Germany. Ten years later it had become the symbol of humiliation. And now it is a term of abuse.

Words are not things. When Smuts pleaded in 1919
for a peace of appeasement he was not asking the weak
to grovel before the strong; he was asking the strong to
show magnanimity and mercy to the weak. In April, he
went to Budapest to negotiate on behalf of the Allies
with the Communist government of Bela Kun and saw
with his own eyes the economic ruin and human misery
of the Danubian countries. The impression left upon him
was indelible.

Nothing so burns up every particle of self as the sights I have passed
through the past week. And this afternoon after I had written to
you, Keynes came to see me and I described to him the pitiful plight
of Central Europe. And he (who is conversant with the finance of
the matter) confessed to me his doubt whether anything really
could be done. Those pitiful people have little credit left, and
instead of getting indemnities from them, we may have to advance
them money to live. And what will Northcliffe and Bottomley and
Beelzebub say? Ah, yes, and what will God say? For there is the
rub.

From this time onwards, Smuts and Keynes were partners
in an all-out campaign for the economic rehabilitation of
Central Europe and a drastic recasting of the Reparation
proposals. Keynes forgave Smuts his blunder—if such it
was—in advising that war pensions and separation allow-
ances could legally be included in the Reparation categories.[1] Smuts came to Keynes for the ammunition he
needed in his furious assault upon the financial and eco-

[1] On this complicated and contentious matter I must content myself here
with quoting a letter which Keynes wrote to Smuts (23 September 1920)
after his 'legal opinion' of 31 March 1919 had been referred to unfavourably
in the *History of the Paris Peace Conference*, edited by H. W. V. Temperley.
'It looks as though they are going to saddle *you* with responsibility for the big
indemnity, which is absolutely unfair, to anyone who knows the facts—
though I am not sure it won't serve you right for writing that memorandum!'

nomic clauses of the draft Treaty. Before long, they found themselves friends.

Poor Keynes often sits with me at night after a good dinner and we rail against the world and the coming flood. And I tell him this is the time for the Griqua prayer (the Lord to come Himself and not send His Son, as this is no time for children). And then we laugh, and behind the laughter is Hoover's terrible picture of 30 million people who must die unless there is some great intervention. But then again we think things are never as bad as that; and something will turn up, and the worst will never be. And somehow all these phases of feeling are true and right in some sense.

It has not been my purpose to inquire to what extent Smuts was right or wrong in any of his detailed criticisms of the Treaty of Versailles or in his wholesale denunciation of it. *The Treaty of Versailles: For and Against*—that would make a splendid series of Wiles lectures, if you find an historian learned and clear-headed enough to deliver them. All that I have done is to give you a few flashlight pictures of the mind of Smuts as he brooded over the condition of Europe and the work of the Peace Conference. They reveal, not the structure and detail of the Treaty, but the perils and agonies of treaty-making. At any rate, they reveal the intense repugnance which Smuts felt to putting his signature to the document.

Then why did he sign it? He had one reason which by itself was compelling. Louis Botha, his prime minister and friend, *had* to sign, for otherwise South Africa would be left in the limbo; she would lose her mandate over German South-West Africa, her membership of the League of Nations, her new status within the Commonwealth and in international law. And how could Smuts separate himself from Botha on issues so critical? He realised, when it came to the point, that to do so would be a betrayal both of his friendship and his political duty. Everybody in South Africa would say that either he or Botha was wrong. He would be splitting the party and ruining all the work of state-building which he and Botha had done in patient and loyal fellowship with each other ever since the Treaty of Vereeniging.

As he fought his battle in those agonising days of late June, Smuts found other reasons for signing. Europe, surely, could not be left stranded on the reef between war and peace. A bad treaty was better than no treaty at all, for it would give Europe at long last the chance of stability and a fresh start. And the League of Nations would be there to help.

Smuts had deeply rooted within him the propensity to hope, which now began to reassert itself over his foreboding. Men might pose and strut on their petty stage and play-act at making history; but all the time a 'dark Figure' was moving the pieces. In optimistic mood, he conceived this Figure to be a benevolent spirit. He called to mind the bitter treaty which he had signed seventeen years ago at Vereeniging. How much of it was left five years later? The defeated Boers were once again ruling their country. Might not something similar happen again?

He began to doubt his own infallibility a little. He had felt so certain of his own wisdom and rectitude while he was addressing his passionate protests to Lloyd George and Wilson; but he now asked himself whether *he* could have done much better than they had done, if *he* had been bearing their responsibilities? He, 'the second representative of South Africa', a man so far removed from the centre of power, a man on the shore shouting advice to men struggling in the water! And when from time to time he had been flung into the water himself, his swimming had not always been competent. He remembered errors of his own and felt that he was no better than the rest of them and must take his place in the dock along with them. Above all, he began to understand the appalling complexity of the task of making peace on the large scale amidst the mental, emotional and material chaos brought about by four years of slaughter and destruction. 'I have really nothing to suggest,' he had written early in May, 'as the dimensions of the problem are beyond me, perhaps beyond human power.'

Twenty years later, it was these sombre reflections, rather than the sanguine ones, which were dominant within his mind. When he carried his country with him into the Second World War, he had no vision of a brave new world to be built upon the ruins of Hitler's world. On 6 September 1939 he wrote to an American friend who had shared with him the hopes and forebodings of the Paris Peace Conference:

Shall we never learn the lesson? There is no solution through war. This war, whatever the ultimate issue, will be followed by another peace which may be no peace, for after a devastating conflict there is no mood for a real and wise peace, as you and I found at Paris in 1919. Meanwhile civilisation is falling back and the light of the spirit is being dimmed. . . . And so the caravan passes once again into the night. May God be with us and take the hands of His erring children.

His mood was the same as the war approached its close.

The hopes of 1919 [he wrote in March 1945] have long ago disappeared. The world has drunk another cup, and it has been a deeper and bitterer cup than the last one. . . . We see a world in ruins, and a victory which, however welcome, cannot remove the sense of loss and ruin which has overtaken us. . . . Still, even in this shipwreck, we have to cling to the small spar of hope which may carry us to the shore beyond this storm.

These lectures are historical, not biographical, in their method and theme. Biography, from time to time, will give me a good deal of help; but I can hardly expect it to do again what it has done today—to do almost my whole job for me.

On the problems that I set out to probe in this lecture I can see very little which I think worth adding to what Smuts felt and thought as he took stock of his experience. The movement from war to peace is, as he discovered, a laborious, complicated, perilous endeavour. Under certain conditions, and particularly when the war has been a localised struggle between two belligerents, the endeavour may contain creative opportunities: Smuts discovered such opportunities in the history of his own country after Vereeniging and in later years he pursued the opportunities further, not only in South Africa but in Ireland and India, in the Commonwealth and the League. Even so, the Anglo-Boer War left behind it a curse which tormented him to the end of his life and torments his country still.

Wars on the European or world scale cannot possibly have a creative outcome. At least, not in this century. Looking back a hundred years from Paris to Vienna, Smuts found some reasons for believing that the statesmen of that time had found it easier to make a just and durable peace.[1] But the statesmen of our own time have found themselves incapable of coping with the chaos, particularly the mental and moral chaos, which total war creates.

From these reflections two questions arise. First: is it permissible to hope that a tolerable passage to peace may someday be found from what we call the Cold War? I think it right to cling to 'the small spar of hope'. The Cold War, after all, is an inaccurate phrase. We might just as well call it the Armed Peace. It falls halfway between peace and war—an uncomfortable and dangerous state, but better by far than being swept away in the flood. We must not deny to human intelligence the prospect of pulling itself upwards, inch by inch, on to the shore of survival.

The second question will be the theme of my next lecture. Let me introduce it by quoting Smuts once again. On 3 June 1919 he wrote to one of his pacifist friends: 'The last battle of the war is being fought out at Paris and we look like losing it. That would appear to justify the views you have held all through of its futility.' Coming as they did from so fierce a fighter, these were astonishing words. They meant that Smuts was casting doubt upon the validity of almost everything that he had done since August 1914. And they prompt us to ask the question: Does non-violence offer an alternative to military preparedness?

---

[1] Smuts, in 1919, had begun by fearing that the Paris Conference would be like the Congress of Vienna; but before long he found himself fearing that it would *not* be like it.

CHAPTER III

NON-VIOLENCE

IN this chapter it is Gandhi who will be my main prop. Even as I write this I realise my presumption, for I have barely touched the fringe of Gandhian studies. The government of India proposes to collect Gandhi's scattered writings in an edition of 73 volumes—no less— whereas my reading, adding one piece to another, would amount scarcely to half a dozen. All the same, I do not believe that Gandhi's complete works, and all the memoirs of his disciples, and all the biographies of him that have so far been written are sufficient, by themselves, to put historians properly on the track of understanding what he attempted and achieved. They do not go beyond the monologue. But his life, surely, was dialogue? Conflict, if you prefer it. Without conflict, what would be his significance in history? We need to understand how he conceived conflict and how he conducted it. But this we shall never do if we forget that conflict is invariably a two-way thing—the tension of ideas, the clash of wills: in its creative moments, the meeting of minds.

I have been studying the conflict of Gandhi with Smuts —the most significant conflict, perhaps, of his whole life, for it was then that he discovered his technique. I underline both the noun and the verb. *Technique*: if Gandhi contributed anything at all to the practice and theory of politics, it was precisely that. He possessed no ideology; nor did he envisage, as most revolutionaries have done,

one specific end that would close the conflict once and for all and in doing so justify the means. On the contrary: he believed that the end was contained within the means and would be *discovered*, for good or bad, in the course and character of the conflict. As your means are, so will your ends be also. Moreover, the means themselves remained always the object of experiment, of discovery. Gandhi discovered his technique as he practised it; his codes of practice, provisional as they always remained, came later.

Throughout his life, the unexpected was a constant element of his experience: never more so than in 1893, the year of his first journey to South Africa. The idea had not as yet entered his head that he was destined for a life of political conflict, in South Africa or anywhere else. Two years earlier, on his return home from London as a qualified barrister, he had had no higher ambition than to earn the means of maintaining his family and repaying his brother the expense of his English education; but he was too awkward and tongue-tied even to achieve that. It was a great stroke of luck for him when his brother secured for him an invitation to go to South Africa and take part in a court case involving two rich and litigious Indians in Paul Kruger's republic.[1]

No sooner had he landed in South Africa than things began to happen to him. He discovered himself face to face with racial discrimination. On the day of his dis-

---

[1] What follows is based chiefly upon Gandhi's two autobiographical books, *The Story of my Experiments with Truth* (Ahmedabad, 2nd ed., 1940) and *Satyagraha in South Africa* (Ahmedabad, 1928). I have also used my own *Survey of British Commonwealth Affairs*, Oxford, 1937, vol. I, ch. IV, for background and for the blue-book evidence.

embarkation at Durban he visited a magistrate's court and was ordered to take off his turban; rather than submit to this affront he left the court and saw himself next day advertised in the newspapers as 'an unwelcome visitor'. On his journey from Durban to Pretoria (in those days it was by rail and road) he was pushed about by the ticket collector on the train and pushed about again by the driver of the coach. In Pretoria he was pushed from the pavement into the gutter. His white tormentors, if only they had known it, were pushing him into politics, with consequences incalculable for the history of South Africa, of India and the world.

Not that he felt resentful. He felt puzzled. He wanted to know whether these things happened only to him or to other Indians also? And if so, why? His shyness slipped away from him and he found himself calling meetings to discuss the situation of the Indian community in the Transvaal. Not that he had any plans for action; it was still his intention to leave South Africa as soon as his legal work was finished; indeed, he was on the very eve of taking ship from Durban when he heard by accident that the Natal legislature was about to debate a franchise bill which would exclude Indians from voting on the grounds of race. Then and there he decided to cancel his passage and to organise a petition to the legislature against the bill. That decision marked his entry into politics.

Here I must pause for a moment to recall how the Indians came to be living in South Africa and the laws under which they were living. The first Indians had come under the system of indentured labour, which was the sequel to slave emancipation and to the ensuing famine of plantation labour throughout the British Empire. The system had been tried out, first in Mauritius, then in the West Indies and later in other places, including Natal. The English abolitionists of the 1830's had suspected it to be the reintroduction of slavery under another name; but they and their successors in England and India were given reassuring promises by Her Majesty's government. They were told that the labourers would receive fair and equal treatment when their indentures expired; that they would be, as Lord Salisbury put it in 1875, 'in all respects free men, with privileges no whit inferior to any other class of Her Majesty's subjects resident in the Colonies'. In the tropical territories, which were destined to remain for a long time under Crown Colony government, this pledge could be made good; but it could not be made good in the territories of white settlement which were advancing rapidly towards self-government. The white settlers had been insistent upon importing Indian labourers to help them out of their economic troubles; they were no less insistent upon denying to these labourers—and to the 'free settlers' who followed in their wake—those opportunities of political, economic and social advancement which they claimed for themselves. They had begun by treating the Indians as human instruments; they continued by resenting them as economic competitors; they ended by imposing upon them a status of legal and political inferiority.

This became the general rule in each of the four South African territories except Cape Colony; but the definition of status differed from territory to territory. In the Orange Free State, Indians were debarred by law from farming, from trading, from every kind of work except the most menial; but in practice this hardly mattered because there was only a handful of Indians resident in the Free State. In the Transvaal, where Indians were resident in considerable numbers, they were debarred by law from citizenship and land ownership and were compelled to pay a registration fee of £3 and give their finger-prints before being allowed to trade. The British government regarded these discriminatory laws and regulations as a violation of the London Convention of 1884 and addressed high-minded protests to President Kruger's government. But meanwhile the same impulses of racial discrimination were at work next door in Natal, under the British flag. To begin with there was the franchise bill of 1894, which became the occasion of Gandhi's entry into politics. There followed later in the year a taxation bill, which had the avowed object of driving the indentured labourers back to India upon the conclusion of their indentures by imposing upon them a tax which they could not possibly pay—£25, which was more than the annual earnings of many of them. A few years later, a bill was introduced into the Natal legislature with the object of putting a full stop to Indian immigration.

In 1894, when he began his fight against this discriminatory legislation, Gandhi founded the Natal Indian Congress as a means of organising opinion not merely in the colony but also in India and Britain. To some extent, his efforts were successful. The Secretary of State refused to sanction the principle of racial discrimination in the franchise and immigration bills, leaving it to the white legislators to achieve their purposes by a different form of words. Gandhi made no protest against that; his only concern at that time was with the principle. For this very reason, the reduction of the tax on Indian labourers from the proposed £25 to £3 did not satisfy him; whatever the figure might be, a tax embodying the principle of racial discrimination admitted no compromise. In the years ahead, a great deal was to be heard about the £3 tax.

All the same, what most impresses one in Gandhi's attitude at this time is its extraordinary moderation. He was able to understand and even to sympathise with the white settlers' repugnance to the Indians on the ground of their low standards of living, their insanitary and untidy habits, their alien culture. In 1896, when he went to India on a six-months' visit, he took pains to point out that the Indians in Natal had duties to perform as well as rights to win. 'My experience has shown me,' he declared, 'that we can win justice quickest by doing justice to the other side.'[1] Unfortunately, the newspapers did not report words such as these but only the criticisms which he made of the white man's laws. These infuriated the white people of Natal; when Gandhi returned to Durban, a gang of white toughs assaulted him and came close to lynching him. He asked God to give him the courage and the sense to forgive them and 'to refrain from bringing them to law'. Already he was discovering the principle of self-suffering, which lay at the root of his technique; but many years were still to pass before he discovered and employed the technique itself. The achievements and potentialities of British justice still seemed to him far greater than its imperfections, and when the Boer

[1] *My Experiments*, p. 225.

War broke out he organised an Indian ambulance corps and served with it under fire around Spion Kop. His main energies as a reformer throughout these years were directed chiefly to self-improvement within his own community. This was a leading theme of the newspaper, *Indian Opinion*, which he founded in 1904. By way of practical demonstration, he shifted the production of the paper to Phoenix Farm, about fourteen miles outside Durban, and established there a community based on the principles of simple living and manual labour. (He made it his own special task to clean the latrines.)

In these and other ways he was making ready, though he might not know it, for the conflict which awaited him. It was precipitated by the British conquerors of the Transvaal. As has been seen, Great Britain had protested, before the war, against the treatment meted out there to the Indians; but, after the war had been won, her servants in the Transvaal forgot these protests or deliberately disregarded them.[1]

Where President Kruger had chastised the Indians with whips, Lord Milner and Lord Selborne and their young men chastised them with scorpions. These servants of the Imperial idea were, in their way, very efficient. The Boers had been too slipshod or too good-natured to enforce the discriminatory laws drastically; but the British set up a new Asiatic Department to make their observance watertight. The officials of this department discovered in the course of time that they needed new legislation to stop

[1] The Lieutenant-Governor of the Transvaal wrote on 13 April 1904: 'Promises have been made without knowledge or perception of the consequences involved in their fulfilment.' He went on to enlarge upon the danger of a 'horde' of Asiatics overrunning the country. Cd. 2339 of 1904, pp. 28 ff.

the leaks. They believed that there were many Indians illegally resident in the Transvaal and that their numbers were constantly being added to. Their remedy for this state of affairs was the Asiatic Law Amendment Ordinance of 1906—the Black Ordinance, as the Indians called it. Its purpose was to close the Transvaal against new Indian immigration and to clear out the illegal immigrants: its method was to compel every Indian—man, woman and child—to take out a new certificate of registration marked by his fingerprints, to carry it on his person and to produce it on the demand of any official or policeman. According to Gandhi, this code was far more stringent, both in its prohibitions and its penalties, than the pass-laws imposed upon the African population of South Africa or the drastic laws directed against the criminal tribes of India.

Gandhi had just been on service with an Indian ambulance unit in the so-called Zulu rebellion of 1906. What he had seen there had impressed upon him the distinction between the principles of British justice, in which he continued to believe, and their perversions. He now felt himself called upon to resist the perversions embodied in the Black Ordinance. On 11 September 1906 he summoned a meeting of Indians in Johannesburg to vote upon four resolutions condemning the Black Ordinance. The fourth resolution became a pledge which the meeting adopted with unanimity. Each man bound himself 'not to submit to the Ordinance in the event of its becoming law in the teeth of their opposition and to suffer all the penalties attaching to their non-submission'.[1]

[1] *Satyagraha*, p. 102.

'Not to submit': these words have the ring of revolution. 'To suffer': these words proclaim a new revolutionary technique. It was a technique which Europeans would find hard to take seriously until it had demonstrated its efficacy in action. A benevolent magnate of Johannesburg, Mr Hoskens, revealed the depth of European misunderstanding at a public meeting which he called on the Indians' behalf. Introducing Gandhi to the meeting, he declared that the Indians had had recourse to 'passive resistance' because they had no other means of resistance. They had no arms. They had no votes. They were few in number. They were weak. They had taken to passive resistance as the weapon of the weak. Gandhi listened with astonishment to this travesty of his thought and instead of delivering the speech which he had prepared stood up to contradict his chairman. He denied that the Indians were passive. He denied that they were weak. They were active and strong. The force which they proposed to use was the strongest force of all. Gandhi called it 'soul force' and contrasted it with that inferior instrument of conflict, 'brute force'.

He felt that the words 'passive resistance' were apt to give rise to a terrible misunderstanding and looked about for a different and distinctive name for the non-violent use of force. He opened a competition in his newspaper and awarded the prize to a competitor who proposed the name *Sadagraha*. He changed this into *Satyagraha*, which for him contained the following meaning: 'Truth (*Satya*) implies love, and firmness (*Agraha*) engenders and therefore serves as a synonym of force. I therefore began to call the Indian movement "Satyagraha", that is to say, the

Force which is born of Truth and Love or non-violence.'[1]

These two sentences have provided much material for many skilled and pertinacious commentators, both philological and philosophical.[2] I dare not seek enrolment in this band of scholars. Still, I must make my own attempt, clumsy though it will be, to read Gandhi's mind about the use of force in those two manifestations of it which he recognised: on the one hand brute force or violent force, on the other hand soul force or non-violent force. He believed, I feel sure, that the use of force must be governed and justified by *satya*, truth. In the tradition of his people, he believed in absolute, total truth as the goal of human striving. He did *not* believe that it is given to any human individual to apprehend this truth; but individual men can and do discover those partial truths that mark the journey of mankind towards the goal. Whenever a man discovers such a truth he must stand by it; he can do no other. But supposing he encounters an enemy who denies this truth and seeks to destroy it? He must resist the enemy. Conflict will then arise between the two men. Conflict for what purpose? So that the truth shall prevail. Conflict of what kind? Of the kind most efficient for achieving the end in view. This end has already been defined—that the truth shall prevail. Truth prevails by getting itself accepted. Particularly does it prevail when the enemy himself accepts it. The object of the conflict is to change the enemy's mind—or, if the enemy has also discovered a partial

[1] *Satyagraha*, p. 109.
[2] The commentators introduce (as Gandhi himself did) a third word, *ahimsa* (from the root *hins*, to kill or injure), signifying non-violence or, more positively, love.

truth, to achieve a synthesis of the two truths through a meeting of the two minds. This, surely, involves discussion. Brute force, violent force, closes the discussion. Soul force, non-violent force, keeps the discussion open. If the enemy uses brute force he must be met with soul force. For the purpose in view—that the truth shall prevail—non-violence is more efficient than violence. Gandhi once declared that the *rishis*, who discovered the law of non-violence in the midst of violence, were greater geniuses than Newton and greater soldiers than Wellington.[1]

Gandhi hated cowardice. He said that, were the choice only between cowardice and violence, he would advise violence. He even admitted that there might at times be no alternative choice. He once told his eldest son that it would have been his duty to use physical force in defence of his father had he been present when the attempt was made, in 1908, to assassinate him. This admission, when one looks at it closely, is a very large one—a gate which might admit to justification many violent revolutions and wars. But usually Gandhi clung close to the rule of non-violence. Not only was it more efficient; it took more courage. To suffer, but not to submit, meant the pitting of one's whole soul against the tyrant.

It goes somewhat against my conscience as an historian to generalise on this heroic scale about Gandhi's doctrine of non-violence. In my attempt to distil the essence of his thought I have had in mind things that he said at many

[1] *Selected Writings of Mahatma Gandhi*, selected and edited by Ronald Duncan, London, 1951, pp. 54–5.

different periods of his life and I have slurred over some contradictions which puzzle me. A good historian does not do these things: on the contrary, he makes it his constant endeavour to study each significant statement in its individual context of time, place and circumstance. Well, I must make what amends I can. Let me now return to Gandhi's action and thought in their specific South African context.

As we have seen, *Satyagraha* was born on 11 September 1906, the day the Indians took the oath at their meeting in Johannesburg not to submit to the Black Ordinance, should it become the law of the land, and to suffer all the penalties arising from their non-submission. Gandhi did his best to prevent it becoming the law of the land. For this reason he went to London to petition the Secretary of State. With his right hand, the Secretary of State made a noble gesture; but with his left hand he made a movement which was clean contrary in its intent. While he was advising the King to disallow the Black Ordinance, he was also telling the political leaders of the Transvaal that he would *not* give the same advice should their parliament, which was due to meet very soon under the new constitution, pass legislation in precisely the same terms. And so it came to pass. Within a few months the Black Ordinance became the Black Act, with force of law as from 1 July 1907. When that day arrived, the government found itself face to face with 7,000 or more Indians, who had deliberately left themselves unregistered in defiance of the law.

From this point onwards the drama unfolds in the form of a dialogue between Gandhi and Smuts. It has already been made quite clear that Smuts bore no original responsibility for the drastic anti-Indian code, which was his *damnosa hereditas* from Crown Colony government; but he had made no attempt to resist, and may even have endorsed the passionate advocacy of the code which was almost universal among the white electorate. But now he felt the weight of his responsibility as Botha's right-hand man in the new government. What could the government do with those 7,000 disobedient Indians? It had assumed the legal right to deport them. But could it deport them all? Or could it prosecute them in the courts and have them all sent to prison? Or could it send the heads of families to prison and leave the women and children to starve? Smuts began to ask himself whether all the provisions of the Act were prudent and just. He put the question to Lord Selborne, who admitted—rather late in the day, for the original responsibility was his— that some of the provisions were far too drastic and ought to be amended: all the same, the Asiatic was 'a very bad person to run away from' and it would be inconsistent with the dignity of the government and parliament to repeal the Act: possibly some compromise might be found along the line of voluntary registration, provided always that the first move came from the Indians.

From his old friend, John X. Merriman, Smuts received a more forthright opinion. Merriman hated the vexatious regulations and the memories which they called up 'of the yellow cap of the Jew or the harrying of the Moriscoes by Spain'. He feared the alienation of liberal opinion in England and the damage that would be done to the British position in India. He suggested a line of retreat whereby the obnoxious provisions would be withdrawn but the substance of the legislation—immigration restriction and registration as the means of enforcing it —would be maintained with the assent of the Indians.

This advice did not help Smuts very much because the whole Act was obnoxious to the Indians and they were demanding, not its amendment, but its total repeal. Meanwhile, Smuts could not escape his responsibility for maintaining the law of the land as it stood. He did so by 'striking at the head', that is, by prosecuting the most prominent resisters. By the end of the year, about 150 of them, including Gandhi, were in gaol. But Smuts held himself ready for a settlement by agreement. So did Gandhi. Through the mediation of one of the Johannesburg editors a meeting was arranged between the two men at the end of January 1908.[1]

Gandhi left that meeting a free man and a happy one. He called his people together and told them that he had reached an honourable understanding with General Smuts, that the Black Act would be repealed and that the Indians could now register themselves voluntarily without suffering any stigma. But some of the Indians felt that Gandhi was being tricked by Smuts. On 10 February, the day fixed for voluntary registration, Gandhi was set upon and severely beaten by two Pathans as he was leading his people to the Registration Office. He was taken to the house of a Baptist clergyman and had the registration official brought to him there so that he might still

[1] The printed documentary evidence for what follows, on Gandhi's side, is contained in the two autobiographies; on Smuts's side in *Legislation Affecting Asiatics in the Transvaal*, Cd. 4327 of 1908.

be the first to register. Most of the Indians followed his example and registration was almost complete by 9 May 1908, the stipulated closing date.

By that time, however, it was becoming clear that Gandhi and Smuts held different interpretations of their agreement. Setting aside the subsidiary points, Gandhi asserted that Smuts had given him a promise to have the Black Act repealed. Smuts denied this. Gandhi thereupon accused Smuts of a breach of faith. The two men were at cross-purposes with each other. Smuts, in protesting his good faith, took his stand upon the documents; Gandhi, in impugning it, relied chiefly upon his interpretation of the conversation. The documents consisted of Gandhi's letter to Smuts of 28 January and a reply from Smuts's secretary next day; the conversation took place on 30 January.

The documents contain no agreement to repeal the Act. In his letter of 28 February, Gandhi underlined the Indian objection to the compulsive element of the Act and explained how registration could be achieved—indeed, achieved more effectively—under the voluntary principle; but he also said:

We recognise that it is not possible during the Parliamentary recess to repeal the Act, and we have noted your repeated public declarations that there is no likelihood of the Act being repealed.

The reply next day on Smuts's behalf by his secretary was brief and businesslike. It left the way open for voluntary registration, provided it was in a form similar to that laid down in the Act; but the only promise it contained was to 'lay the matter before Parliament at its next session'.

If Smuts had believed that a more far-reaching agreement emerged from his talk next day with Gandhi he would surely have had it set down in writing. But Gandhi's temperament and habits were different. Throughout his whole life he set very little store upon official documents—even the most important documents, such as the Government of India Act, 1935, which he left unread until many years had passed[1]—but he always set the greatest store upon personal encounters. We cannot doubt that he took his farewell of Smuts on 30 February 1908 in the sincere belief that their encounter had ended in a victory for his cause. But no more can we doubt that Smuts, with equal sincerity, believed the opposite. Imprecision and optimism were at the root of the misunderstanding between the two men.

Many years later, when Gandhi committed to writing his memories of that year, he was fair-minded enough to put a question mark after the words 'breach of faith.' But at the time he admitted no such doubt and almost certainly felt none. He told his people that he had been tricked and that the fight was on again—not merely against the Registration Act, but against the Immigration Restriction Act which had followed it. The renewal of battle was signalised at a great meeting in Johannesburg on 16 August, when more than 2,000 Indians burnt the certificates of registration which they had voluntarily taken out.

While Gandhi was accusing Smuts of breaking faith, Smuts was accusing Gandhi of raising a new issue.

[1] My authority for this statement is a letter dated 13 July 1941 from Lord Linlithgow, then Viceroy of India, to Smuts.

Hitherto, the Indians had made no protest against the principle of immigration restriction. But how could they have made any protest, retorted Gandhi, until the principle was embodied in legislation? To Smuts, this argument must have appeared casuistical. He called Gandhi 'cunning'.

But let us look at the problem as Gandhi saw it. On his premises, it was not only logical but also inevitable that a battle which had been joined for the sake of strictly limited objectives should grow into a battle for wider objectives.

My experience has taught me [he wrote later] that a law of progress applies to every righteous struggle. As the Ganga advances, other streams flow into it, and hence at the mouth it has grown so wide that neither bank is to be seen and a person sailing upon the river cannot make out where the river ends and the sea begins. So also as a Satyagraha struggle progresses onward, many another current helps to swell its current, and there is a constant growth in the results to which it leads. This really is inevitable, and is bound up with the first principles of Satyagraha. For in Satyagraha the minimum is also the maximum, and as it is the irreducible minimum, there is no question of retreat, and the only movement possible is an advance. . . . The Ganga does not leave its course in search of tributaries. Even so does the Satyagrahi not leave his path which is sharp as the sword's edge. But as the tributaries join the Ganga as it advances, so it is with the river that is Satyagraha.[1]

There was little chance that Smuts, or for that matter any other politician of Western upbringing, would understand reflections such as these without first getting to understand the man who made them. To begin with, the idea that there was no room for bargaining, that there was no chance at all of persuading Gandhi to reduce the

[1] *Satyagraha*, pp. 208–9.

demands which he had originally put forward, was a novel one. Still more puzzling was Gandhi's assertion that his minimum was also his maximum, that he would never add to the demands that he had originally put forward. In attacking immigration restriction he seemed to be doing the opposite! Surely there was a contradiction between what he said he would do and what he did? Gandhi would have admitted no contradiction. It was the government, he would have retorted, that was widening the field of conflict, as an unjust government was bound to do.

Smuts tried his utmost not to widen the field of conflict. As the years went by he acquired some Gandhian skills: for example, he trained his officials and police in the subtle act of *not* putting Indians into gaol. But Gandhi was biding his time, confident that the government would sooner or later give him just cause for renewing the struggle on the grand scale. He had gathered his faithful *Satyagrahis* around him on Tolstoy Farm, a place about twenty miles from Johannesburg, put at his disposal by a well-to-do German South African named Kallenbach. The faithful were a much diminished band, but closely knit together within their community of mutual aid and simple living, a finely tempered *élite* ready to demonstrate the power of non-violence in the approaching struggle.

It was in 1913 that Gandhi saw and took his chance of making *Satyagraha* a mass movement. During the past few years, when his power in South Africa had appeared to be on the wane, he had been broadening its basis overseas, and had won strong support for his cause in Great

Britain and India. Behind the screen of the old constitutional forms, the position of Indians in South Africa was well on its way to becoming a problem of international relations. The Viceroy was voicing the indignant protests of Indian nationalism. The government of the Union was beginning to think that it might do well to have some discussion with a representative of Mother India. In 1912, it invited G. K. Gokhale, the respected leader of moderate Indian nationalism, to come to South Africa.[1]

Gokhale met a good reception everywhere, from the white people as well as the Indians, and, on the eve of his return home in November 1912, he held constructive talks with the government. Their sequel was legislation introduced into parliament early the next year to transfer the regulation of Indian affairs from the Provinces to the Union and at the same time to rationalise and humanise the system. The Transvaal's Black Act, which had been the original occasion of *Satyagraha*, disappeared at long last. The power to restrict Asian immigration was to operate henceforward on economic and social, never on racial grounds. All this, surely, was a great step forward in narrowing the field of conflict? Gandhi would not admit it. By the mere process of consolidating provincial legislation, he argued, the parliament of the Union was committing new aggressions: for example, although in practice it left the Indians of the Free State precisely in the same position as before, it was putting the stamp of national endorsement upon their disabilities. This legalis-

---

[1] The documentary evidence for what follows is contained in the two autobiographies and in *Correspondence Relating to the Immigrants' Regulation Acts,* Cd. 7111 of 1913.

tic argument was unlikely to arouse the masses. Gandhi needed a slogan which would strike right home to their emotions. He found it in the discriminatory £3 tax imposed upon the Indians of Natal nearly twenty years earlier.

Gandhi had not hitherto felt justified in making the £3 tax an objective of his campaign, for that would have taken him beyond 'the maximum' which he had stated. However, he now convinced himself that the government itself had thrown the tax into the arena of conflict. Smuts, he declared, had promised Gokhale that the tax would be repealed. He had broken this promise, just as he had broken his promise in 1908 to repeal the Black Act.

I do not doubt that Gandhi was sincere when he made this accusation, but I can find no more evidence than I found on the earlier occasion that it was well grounded. This time, there was not even an exchange of letters: the only evidence we have is combined in the statements made subsequently by the parties to the controversy. I shall not report or summarise these statements, but shall simply give my own reading of what *probably* happened at the meeting between Gokhale and the ministers. Gokhale, I believe, criticised the £3 tax and asked for its repeal. The ministers listened sympathetically and promised to consider the request favourably, provided they could win the consent of the Natal legislators. Smuts, I think, led Gokhale to believe, as he believed himself, that Natal would 'come quietly'. In the event he was proved wrong. He and his colleagues were probably guilty of raising hopes which they failed to fulfil. They were not guilty of mendacity.

Gandhi himself showed signs, many years later, of
giving them some benefit of the doubt; Gokhale, he
wrote, had 'supposed' that the tax would be repealed.
Between supposition and knowledge there is a wide
gap. But at the time, Gandhi saw everything in black
and white. By breaking its pledge, the government had
committed another wrong and given him just cause for
attacking the £3 tax. Meanwhile, the Supreme Court
of the Cape Province was giving him something else to
attack. One of its judgements (for all I know, it may have
had some grounds in strict law) produced the appalling
effect of invalidating Indian marriages and bastardising
Indian children wholesale. 'As if unseen by anyone,'
Gandhi wrote later, 'God was preparing the ingredients
for the Indians' victory and demonstrating still more
clearly the injustices of the Europeans in South Africa.'[1]

With a brilliant mastery of tactics, Gandhi chose a select
band of women to lead his forces into action. The women
aroused the Indian coal miners at Newcastle in Natal and
they came out on strike. The mineowners cut off their
water and light. Gandhi arrived on the scene and gathered
them by thousands into an open-air camp. But how could
he feed them? He solved this problem by passing it on
to the prison authorities. In the Transvaal they would be
illegal immigrants; Gandhi organised them as an army
of 'pilgrims' and marched them across the border. There
the government arrested them, as it was bound to do. It
also arrested Gandhi, to his great satisfaction. He had by
now fifty thousand Indians ardently seeking arrest. As he
recalled the situation in later life: 'The Union Govern-

[1] *Satyagraha*, p. 273.

ment had not the power to keep thousands of innocent men in gaol. The Viceroy would not tolerate it, and all the world was waiting to see what General Smuts would do.'

Smuts capitulated. I have not the time to follow his steps along the road of capitulation—some of them were very difficult—but they brought him at last to a new conference with Gandhi. This time, he said, there must be no imprecision, no mental reservations or misunderstandings on either side. Everything agreed between them must be written down and tested word by word to make sure that their words were in complete accord with their thoughts. By wrestling thus with each other, they reached at last a firm agreement. It was embodied in the Indian Relief Act of July 1914. Gandhi did not accept this Act as a settlement of all the Indian claims for justice; but he did accept it as a settlement of those specific and limited demands that he had made. He sailed away from South Africa, soon after the outbreak of war, in the knowledge that he had fought and won his seven years' battle with Smuts. We can imagine the sigh of relief which Smuts gave as he wrote: 'The saint has left our shores, I sincerely hope for ever.'

Writing about Gandhi twenty-five years later, Smuts said that South Africa had been his 'training-school'. I shall review briefly the lessons he had learnt in that school and the conditions under which he had learnt them.

I can deal briefly with the lessons, for we have followed Gandhi step by step as he discovered his technique and demonstrated its efficacy. But let me refer you to an excellent book which I have read recently, Dr Joan Bondurant's *Conquest of Violence*.[1] Besides expounding Gandhi's thought in the terms of political philosophy, Dr Bondurant offers a systematic, comparative analysis of five separate campaigns of *Satyagraha* which were fought on Indian soil between 1918 and 1931. In one or other of these campaigns some new weapon may sometimes have been brought into action (in 1939, Smuts took particular note of the fact that Gandhi, while he was in South Africa, had never used the weapon of fasting, or 'self-starvation'), but by and large the most elaborate and successful of these Indian campaigns adds very little to the methods of non-violence which Gandhi had already practised in South Africa. The *Satyagraha* which he brought with him from South Africa to India was already highly developed.

Developed under what conditions? I am not certain that this question has ever before been raised explicitly; but to me it is a very important one. There are two aspects of it which I think particularly deserving of emphasis, first the constitutional aspect and secondly the personal aspect. The Union of South Africa had a constitution of the British type in which the executive government and its instruments, including the police force, were subject to the rule of law. Individuals, even the most troublesome individuals, enjoyed the fundamental liberties of speaking, writing, publishing, petitioning, propagandising. There were open skies for Gandhi's propaganda not

---

[1] Joan V. Bondurant, *Conquest of Violence. The Gandhian Philosophy of Conflict*, Princeton, 1958. See also *Mahatma Gandhi—Political Philosopher?* by W. H. Morris Jones in *Political Studies*, vol. VIII, no. 1.

only in South Africa, but also in India, Great Britain and the whole British Empire. So far as I know, there was no restriction upon his right of appeal to public opinion anywhere in the world. More than anything else, it was the force of public opinion, particularly British and Indian public opinion, that brought Smuts to terms with Gandhi.

There was, moreover, something within Smuts himself which made him receptive of this public opinion and sympathetic towards the man who was inciting it. At first sight, the distance between the Indian and the Boer might seem to be as wide as the distance between East and West; and yet, the more closely one studies their early lives, the more clearly one sees them setting out from their widely separated bases of ancestral custom and belief towards a common meeting ground. If they were born for conflict with each other they were also born to make peace with each other. In their later years this became the settled conviction of both of them.

It was my fate [wrote Smuts in 1939[1]] to be the antagonist of a man for whom even then I had the highest respect. . . . I must frankly admit that his activities at that time were very troublesome to me. Together with other South Africans I was then busily engaged on the task of welding the old Colonies into a unified State. . . . It was a colossal work which took up every moment of my time. Suddenly in the midst of all those engrossing preoccupations Gandhi raised a most troublesome issue. We had a skeleton in our cupboard. . . .

Smuts went on to describe the Indian grievances and the technique which Gandhi invented for getting them re-

---

[1] S. Radhakrishnan (ed.), *Mahatma Gandhi, Essays and Reflections on his Life and Work, presented to him on his seventieth birthday, October 2nd, 1939*, London, 1939. Smuts's contribution is entitled 'Gandhi's Political Method'.

dressed. He told the story of their struggle and of the little personal touches which had kept it sweet—for example, of Gandhi setting to work in prison to make him the pair of sandals which he had worn 'for many a summer since'. Those sandals! Gandhi's biographers like to tell how Smuts returned them to the Mahatma on the occasion of his seventieth birthday; but all he sent was a photograph of them; they were still 'a precious relic' in his own possession on that day, nine years later, when he heard the news of Gandhi's death and exclaimed: 'A prince among men has passed away and we grieve with India in her irreparable loss.'

A similar image of his encounter with Smuts was engraved upon Gandhi's memory. There were times—for example, at the crisis of the Round Table Conference of 1931—when he wrote to Smuts and invoked his aid 'in the cause you rightly believe is the world's cause'. Earlier in the same year, when the Gandhi–Irwin Agreement was being forged, his recollection of Smuts had helped him to get past a dangerous stumbling block. He had demanded drastic restrictions upon the activities of the police and the Viceroy had refused him flatly on grounds of public security. 'Ah,' he exclaimed, 'now Your Excellency treats me like General Smuts treated me in South Africa. You do not deny that I have an equitable claim, but you advance unanswerable reasons from the point of view of Government why you cannot meet it. I drop the demand.'[1]

Not even the political clouds which gathered around South Africa after the Second World War could shake

[1] Earl of Halifax, *Fullness of Days*, London, 1957, p. 148.

the trust and affection that Gandhi felt for Smuts. In 1946, when Mrs Pandit was setting out for the United Nations Assembly under official instructions to make a frontal assault upon the Union's racial policies, she was summoned by Gandhi and told: 'That I should shake your hand and ask your blessing for my cause.'[1]

This chapter is drawing to its close and so far I have not even mentioned the question which I raised at the end of the previous chapter: 'Does non-violence offer an alternative to armed conflict or preparedness for it?' The historian sometimes finds his training a great curse. It commits him to the laborious task of studying ideas as they take shape in action within a specific framework of time, place and circumstance. It commits him to the slow, patient method of case-study. I have the feeling even now that my South African 'case' is an insufficient basis for generalisation: that I ought really to be following Gandhi into India. How different were Indian from South African circumstances? Sociologically, the differences were immense. But politically? From some points of view they were just as large; but not from all points of view. By 1921, Gandhi had come to the conclusion, which he had never reached in South Africa, that the existing system of government in India was wholly bad and utterly incapable of self-improvement. But is this conclusion generally accepted by historians? One is familiar with the angry exclamation, so popular among impatient reactionaries, 'Govern or get out!' The dilemma is seldom so sharp as that. From 1917 onwards Great Britain stood

[1] Nagantara Sahgal, *Prison and Chocolate Cake*, London, 1954, p. 196.

committed in India to the most difficult political task in the world—to govern *while* she was getting out.

No doubt the process of getting out was spun out too long; but in operations of this kind, as African experience has since made clear, the time-factor is always tricky: one can have a bicycle accident either by going too slow or by going too fast. Fast or slow, the switch-over from autocratic government to self-government remained throughout the inter-war years the persistent objective of British policy in India. Did this have any significance for Gandhi? Did he realise that, notwithstanding Amritzar and all the gaolings and lathi charges, his voice could still be heard throughout India and Britain and the whole world, even more clear and loud than in his South African years? Did he really imagine that British constitutionalism, with its imperfections and backslidings, belonged to the same political family as Nazi or Soviet totalitarianism? Did he believe that his technique of non-violence, which had proved its worth in conflict with Smuts and Halifax, would prove just as effective in conflict with Hitler and Stalin?

Gandhi was too honest a man to shirk questions like these. On 26 November 1938 he wrote an article for *Harijan* on the situation of the Jews under the Nazi terror.[1]

Can the Jews resist this shameless and organised persecution? Is there a way to preserve their self-respect, and not to feel helpless, neglected and forlorn? I submit there is. . . . If I were a Jew and were born in Germany and earned my livelihood there, I would

---

[1] *Selected Writings of Mahatma Gandhi*, selected and edited by Ronald Duncan, London, 1951. See pp. 90–3.

claim Germany as my home even as the tallest Gentile might, and challenge him to shoot me or to cast me in the dungeon; I would refuse to be expelled or to submit to discriminating treatment. And for doing this I would not wait for the fellow-Jews to join me in civil resistance, but would have confidence that in the end all were bound to follow my example. If one Jew or all the Jews were to accept my prescription here offered, he or they cannot be worse off than now. And suffering voluntarily undergone will bring them an inner strength and joy which no number of resolutions passed in the world outside Germany can.

So far, you will observe, Gandhi has made no claim such as he made constantly in South Africa and India, that non-violence will achieve a political victory: his argument has taken him quite outside the realm of politics, in that he recommends the Jews to offer non-violent resistance, not for any political advantage they will gain by it, but for the sake of their own moral and spiritual ennoblement. Still, he goes on to argue that they are much better situated than the Indians in South Africa had been to launch a *Satyagraha* campaign and carry it through to victory.

I am convinced that, if someone with courage and vision can arise among them to lead them in non-violent action, the winter of their despair can be turned into the summer of hope. . . . The German Jews will score a lasting victory over the German gentiles in the sense that they have converted the latter to an appreciation of human dignity.

Underlying this sanguine forecast is the assumption that the totalitarian state and the disposition of its leaders make no real difference. Conflict with Hitler and conflict with Smuts are essentially the same thing and will produce the same result. Gandhi admitted that Hitler had a heart harder than stone; but the hardest material, he said, would yield to sufficient heat. I wonder.

There remains considerable room, it seems to me, for speculation about the potentialities and limitations of non-violence in the sphere of domestic conflict.

In the sphere of international conflict, the room for speculation is almost limitless. Gandhi himself never pursued any practical experiments in this sphere. It is true that he commended non-violence to the Czechs after Munich as 'a weapon not of the weak but of the brave'.[1] In 1942 he commended it to his own people, when they were faced with the threat of Japanese invasion. But this was when they were still living under an alien government and one which he believed to be incapable of self-improvement. Supposing they had been living under a government worthy of their respect and devotion? So long as Gandhi retained his faith in the British Empire, he had thought it his duty to offer it his personal service in time of war—in 1899, in 1906, in 1914. And that, he once said, was just how he would expect every Indian to act towards his own country under *Swaraj*.[2]

I should be deeply distressed, if on every conceivable occasion every one of us were to be a law unto oneself and to scrutinise in golden scales every action of our future National Assembly. I would surrender my judgment in most matters to national representatives, taking particular care in my choice of such representatives.

What guidance is to be found in words such as those for the men who now conduct the foreign policy of India? In their dealings with Pakistan, non-violence has

---

[1] *Selected Writings of Mahatma Gandhi*, pp. 86–9.
[2] *Ibid.*, pp. 55–6.

not been conspicuously the rule. Would Gandhi have approved their conduct or disapproved it? Would he have approved or disapproved the attitude they have taken towards the encroachments of China upon India's Himalayan frontier? In answer to these questions, one man's guess would be as good as another's.

In these latter days, it is an Englishman, not an Indian, who has made himself the most forthright advocate of non-violence as a weapon—as *the* weapon—of international conflict. In his book, *Defence in the Cold War*, Sir Stephen King-Hall attacks the central problem of our times, not as a pacifist, but as a militant patriot, ardent for total victory in his country's war of ideas against Soviet Communism. This war, he declares, is being fought here and now and will continue to be fought until one side or the other has stamped its image upon a united world. It is a war which cannot possibly be won by the hydrogen bomb: if we and our allies are bluffing when we say that we shall use it, we risk defeat through having our bluff called: if we are not bluffing and do use it, we shall bring total destruction not only upon the enemy, but upon ourselves, and the very way of life which we are purporting to defend. Nor is it any use hoping to find a halfway house by using the so-called tactical nuclear weapons, for they will put us on the escalator which leads inevitably to H-bomb warfare. The alternative strategy which Sir Stephen King-Hall favours finds its application in the following uncompromising proposals:

(1) to wage political warfare on a large scale and in an aggressive spirit against Communism;

(2) to forego, if necessary by unilateral decision, not only the H-bomb but nuclear weapons of all kinds;

(3) to deny bases on British soil to allies using nuclear weapons, in the knowledge that this will almost certainly involve British withdrawal from NATO;

(4) if possible, to form an association (ETO) with the other nations of western Europe who will similarly forswear nuclear weapons and forbid their use by allies on their soil;

(5) to reduce the 'conventional' forces of Britain (and ETO) to token size;

(6) to make preparation for the eventuality of a Russian occupation of Britain;

(7) to train the British people to defeat the forces of occupation by non-violent combat.

Sir Stephen King-Hall wishes to have his proposals, with their supporting argument, examined by a strong commission of inquiry. I myself have sometimes wondered whether the time is not now ripe for a new Esher committee, or something like it, to examine systematically, realistically and, if need be, ruthlessly, the whole structure of British defence policy and the assumptions on which it has been built.[1] If such a body were set up, I should think it ought to consider the King-Hall proposals along with all the other ones that would be brought forward. But I do not think that the proposals deserve a commission of inquiry all to themselves.

To me, they represent a false conclusion based upon questionable premisses and faulty logic. I question the opening affirmation that we are doomed to fight per-

---

[1] Of course, the government might think that this review could be made just as efficiently without the aid of a specially appointed commission. Others might think that only a committee which is *not* dominated by politicians would show the ruthlessness which is requisite for raising and probing fundamental questions.

petual war against the Communists until either we or they are masters of a united world. Not that I underrate the intensity of the conflict that is now being fought or feel able to forecast its end: but to state dogmatically that it will never end except by overwhelming victory for one side or the other seems to me to have no warrant in probability or historical experience. Civilisation has been rent and tortured before now by passionate conflicts of faith and ideology—by jehads, crusades and wars of religion. All of them came to an end, sooner or later, without overwhelming victory for one side. I dread and dislike this passion for overwhelming victory, and none the less so when it calls itself non-violent. I prefer the more accommodating temperament of Gandhi, or the worldly prudence of Queen Elizabeth who asked to be saved from Sir Francis Walsingham and his 'brethren in Christ' when they wanted her to fight all the Catholics all the time. The world, I think, could do with fewer crusaders and more *politiques*.

Sir Stephen King-Hall believes that political warfare unsupported by military power can win great victories. He is an expert in political warfare; but I have talked with other experts who do not share his confidence. They think that political warfare, when employed at the right time and in the right place, can be a useful *auxiliary* weapon. For myself, I am not convinced that shouting will by itself bring down the walls of Jericho. Anyway, I dislike shouting.

But now I come to the rift of logic in the linked sequence of the King-Hall proposals. It lies between points 4 and 5 of the programme. Up to then, the logic has

moved forward from the premisses without any break.
From an estimate of the significance of nuclear weapons,
substantially the same as that in Mr Brodie's book, it is
quite logical, though not necessarily wise, to proceed to
the advocacy of complete unilateral nuclear disarmament
and, consequentially, the disruption of the Atlantic alliance. But the next step—the near-total *conventional* disarmament of western Europe—does not follow in logic. A
quite extraneous reason is given for putting this proposal
forward: in effect, that the nations of western Europe, although their combined population (not to mention their
wealth) is greater than that of the Russians and their
satellites, lack the will to defend themselves by military
means of any kind. But, if their comforts mean so much
more to them than their freedom, what reason have we
to believe that they will summon up the will to fight the
battle of freedom non-violently? Is it suggested that
non-violent conflict is a cheaper and easier road to victory? Gandhi never fell into that unheroic error.

As to the chances of winning an international conflict
by the methods of non-violence, I have already pointed
out that we have no empirical evidence to go on. Gandhi
speculated a little on the problem but such light as he shed
on it is flickering. You may care to carry the speculations
further. You may ask yourselves how you will go non-
violently into action, in your corner of the United Kingdom, against Russian forces of occupation. Meanwhile,
I, as an Australian, may ask myself how I shall go non-
violently into action against Chinese conquerors. And
we can both be asking ourselves what kind of training
the Russians and Chinese will be giving to the Baganda

and the Papuans and all the other peoples whom we shall desert. Can you still envisage a united world stamped with the image of our freedom? Can Sir Stephen King-Hall still envisage it?

You will notice that I have not discussed the problem from the point of view of the convinced pacifist. I have not been able to find a book which bridges the gap between pacifist ethics and international politics, or even attempts to bridge it. I should like to see the attempt made.

Finally, let me note that it would take ten years or thereabouts, under the King-Hall programme, to organise and train the British nation for non-violent conflict. The training has not yet begun. Since I am writing in the indicative, not the optative mood, I can only conclude that non-violence is not at present an alternative to violence as a means of achieving victory in international conflict. Nor is it an alternative to military power as a means of deterring aggression and reducing the risk of suicidal war.

CHAPTER IV

CIVITAS MAXIMA

THIS study is focused upon international society. I have found the subject difficult to treat concisely, and you may find it hard to follow unless I tell you at the beginning what its method and arrangement are. Most of the time, but not all of it, I shall be standing at some distance from the wood, trying to see its general shape. I shall begin by looking at international society as it appears (or as I think it appears) to international lawyers of different types and temperaments. After that I shall get in amongst the trees in order to pick up the Commonwealth path about halfway through the First World War and follow it until it joins the League of Nations path. Then I shall come outside the wood again and try to get a general view, first of the Commonwealth and the League in the period 1919–39, secondly of the Commonwealth and the United Nations in the period 1945–60. I shall conclude the study with an attempt to lengthen the perspective in which I have hitherto been presenting the problems of war and peace in this century.

Lawyers have given various names—MAGNA COM-MUNITAS, MAGNA SOCIETAS, CIVITAS MAXIMA—to the international community which they have envisaged. I choose the last name, partly because I like the sound of it, partly because the sense of it was conveniently cloudy to the man who popularised it. He was Christian Wolff, a superficial and long-winded philosopher of natural law, whose chief claim to fame is that he played some part in the education both of Vattel and of Immanuel Kant. We might, perhaps, have expected to find his name recorded on the role of honour which commemorates those men of generous aspiration—the Abbé St Pierre, Kant, Smuts, Wilson—who have envisaged a new international polity within which the nations of the world may live in peace with each other. But nothing of the kind: Wolff was quite satisfied with the existing arrangement of sovereign states in which his own Prussia felt so much at home. His CIVITAS MAXIMA had no constitutional or political content. It was merely a postulate of reasoning.

It is interesting to see the changes which international lawyers have been ringing during the past four centuries upon the old tag, *ubi societas ibi ius.* To the founding fathers of the sixteenth century it seemed self-evident that the international community, in some form or another, exists: consequently (since every community has its law) international law must also exist. But by the time we have reached the eighteenth century this reasoning has been turned upside down: international law, says Wolff, exists: consequently, the international community must also exist. This line of reasoning has found favour with some eminent international lawyers of our own century. Lauterpacht takes it as his hypothesis that the will of the international community must be obeyed; Kelsen proves by pure theory that international law is superior to the law of the state. There are, however, other lawyers of equal ability, such as de Visscher and Corbett, who find this reasoning too abstract. To postulate the existence of

CIVITAS MAXIMA, they say, is to take for granted the very
thing which needs to be demonstrated.

The matter of immediate contention in these contro-
versies is the binding character—indeed, the very existence—of international law. Here is a great Serbonian bog
into which I dare not let myself sink. I take my stand, an
inexpert onlooker, on the fringes of juristic speculation,
hoping to find a little help towards answering some
questions which sorely puzzle me. Does the international
community exist, not only in theory but also in reality?
If so, what kind of community is it? Where has it come
from and whither is it going?

The different answers which different lawyers give to
questions such as these seem to me to have their roots in
differences, not merely of intellect but also of temperament. I find some writers temperamentally sanguine,
others temperamentally sombre. Among the former I
would put Mr C. Wilfred Jenks, whose book, *The
Common Law of Mankind*,[1] I have read recently. Ten
learned papers on such widely separated problems as
world organisation, colonial policy, employment policy,
atoms for peace, the exploitation of Antarctica and the
exploration of outer space are illuminated and unified by
a central concept, namely:

. . . the concept that we have outlived the phase in the development of international law when the law could properly be envisaged
as the rules governing the mutual relations of sovereign States in
peace and war and must now, if we are to consolidate the striking
achievements of the last generation and lay a firm foundation for
future development, be guided by the general principle that inter-

[1] London, 1948.

national law can be intelligently expounded and rationally developed
only if it is regarded as the common law of mankind in an early
stage of its development.[1]

Of course, I am completely unqualified to take part in
the professional discussion to which this argument invites
the lawyers; but I can give my impression of its tempera-
mental overtones. The sentence which I have quoted has
some words of caution at the end; but The Common Law
of MANKIND is printed on the title-page and the outer
spine of the book without any qualification. To me it
has the ring of a manifesto. And I get the impression,
from the sentence that I have quoted, that international
law has been getting a move on recently and is now
gathering its strength for a great leap forward. I get the
same impression from successive chapters of the book—
for example, from the chapter entitled 'The Impact of
International Organisation on International Law'. True,
the world has recently suffered some setbacks, such as the
First World War, the collapse of the League of Nations,
the Second World War and the Cold War; but if international lawyers keep their sense of perspective they will
realise that there is no need for them to be discouraged.
Mr Jenks invites them to look back to 1914, to call to
mind all the progress that has been made since then and
count their blessings. In 1914 violence was legal; now it
is not. In 1914 there existed no permanent international
judicature; now it exists. In 1914 it was difficult to make
international law by legislative action; now it is much
easier. In 1914 international custom grew slowly; now
it grows quite fast. In 1914 there was no secular arm to

[1] *Op. cit.*, p. 1.

enforce international law; now we see the secular arm enforcing it in places like Korea and Suez. In 1914 there was no international protection of civil rights; we are changing that now.[1]

Although he does not ignore the black cloud of terror and suffering which has hung over humanity ever since 1914, Mr Jenks is more intent upon the cloud's silver lining. To him it is far more glittering than any silver lining that I can see. The reason, I suppose, is that he, as a lawyer, feels able and perhaps obliged to develop his professional thought as a relatively self-contained system; whereas I, as an historian, feel unable to envisage the development of international law except in the social and economic, the strategical and political contexts of our time.

Lawyers of a more sombre (or sober) temperament seem to feel the same difficulty that I feel. Professor Charles de Visscher of Brussels and Professor P. E. Corbett of Princeton, whose names I mentioned just now, seem determined to insist, if not to over-insist, upon the inextricable entanglement of international law with the politics of sovereign states. They proclaim, even in choosing the titles of their books, their firm determination to keep their legal feet upon the political ground.[2]

In his latest book, Professor Corbett is less concerned with the thought of international lawyers than with the thoughts and deeds of the governments who employ

[1] *Op. cit.*, pp. 174–6.
[2] Charles de Visscher, *Theory and Practice in Public International Law* (trans. from the French by P. E. Corbett), Princeton, 1957; P. E. Corbett, *Law and Society in the Relations of States*, New York, 1957, and *Law in Diplomacy*, Princeton, 1959.

them. The employment is plentiful, for the invocation of legal rules has been for some centuries past a commonplace of diplomacy. Does not this imply that governments recognise the existence of a legal order within which their claims must be tested and determined? Unfortunately, governments have been apt to insist upon their own interpretations of the rules of this legal order to a degree which makes it almost intolerably subjective. The complaint is frequently heard nowadays that the Communist states use international law as a weapon in their political struggle against other states; but this, says Corbett, is nothing new. He calls to mind the twists and turns of British legal argumentation about the rights of passage at sea and of American legal argumentation about the recognition of revolutionary governments. The lawyers of Queen Elizabeth argued for *mare liberum* against the Spaniards; the lawyers of her successors upheld *mare clausum* against the Dutch. United States lawyers found good reasons for upholding the principle of self-determination in Texas and Panama, cynical as its manipulation had been in those places; but they saw no good reason why the same principle should prevail in the Confederate South. Are we to conclude from experience such as this that international law is as long as Queen Elizabeth's foot, or Theodore Roosevelt's foot, or Stalin's foot?[1]

According to Corbett, such a conclusion would be too

---

[1] *Law in Diplomacy*, pp. 11–15, 55–6, 67–82. Corbett notes that Theodore Roosevelt, who engineered the Panama coup, claimed 'a mandate from civilisation' and was supported by the most eminent of American international lawyers, John Bassett Moore, who declared that America was doing a work, 'not only for itself but for mankind'. He asks whether an international lawyer might not also consider respect for treaty obligations a service to mankind?

extreme. Governments conduct much of their business with each other in accordance with regular patterns of practice which are approved by some kind of 'consensus' to which they are all parties. These patterns of practice influence their conduct: that is to say, they have a normative character. But do they extend over a sufficient range and possess sufficient authority to justify their description as a system of law? Unfortunately, their efficacy reaches its maximum in the zone of minor interests and falls to its minimum in the zone of major interests; where a Great Power believes that its vital interests are at issue, it falls to zero. This leads de Visscher to lament the insincerity (*Geist der Unwahrheit*) which has been made a just reproach against international law. It leads Corbett, much against his original inclination, to assert that international law does not exist. To treat the patterns of international practice as a system of law, he declares, leads to wasteful self-deception and a misdirection of energy. He prefers to start from the assumption 'that the international sphere, not being one where any overall constitutional authority reigns, is not in principle a realm of law'. But, if it is not a realm of law, neither can it be a real community. *Ius* and *societas* stand or fall together. This is important not merely theoretically, but also practically. We shall get into a muddle, says Corbett, both in discussing foreign policy and in conducting it, if we mistake our wishes for reality; if we fail to face the fact that the disjunctive forces in international life are far stronger than the conjunctive forces, and that men will have to accept profound changes in the authority which they ascribe to the state, and in the claims which they make upon it, before a real international community can come into existence. This, by and large, is also de Visscher's conclusion. The international community, he says, is a potential order in the minds of men but not yet an effectively established order. Let us think of it as 'a civilising idea'.[1]

I have made no attempt—how could I?—to act as an adjudicator in the controversy. It is not for the layman to tell the members of a neighbouring profession that they need, or do not need, to call themselves by a new name and generally to change their habits of speech and thought. Perhaps I have shown some preference for the sombre rather than the sanguine interpreters; if so, it is because I have the historian's habit of looking at law as a thing contained within a social and political framework.

In practice, the sanguine and the sombre writers seem to be generally in agreement upon the line of advance that needs to be followed in the immediate future. They appear equally anxious to expand and strengthen the existing network of international organisation.

Viewed from the outside, the network is quite impressive—CIVITAS MAXIMA in *posse*, if not yet in *esse*. At the centre of the network is the United Nations Organisation which, like the League of Nations before it, aspires to universality both in its membership and its range of interest: high politics on the world scale. The other organisations are limited, either functionally or regionally. The Specialised Agencies, like their precursors the Technical Unions, are functional in their intention.

[1] De Visscher, *op. cit.*, pp. 88–90, 98–100, 289–91. Corbett, *Law and Society*, pp. 8–12; *Law in Diplomacy*, pp. viii, 273.

NATO and its kindred elsewhere are regional organisations which seem to belong to the family of the *Kriegsverein*. The European Economic Community is a regional organisation which seems to belong to the family of the *Zollverein*.

The Commonwealth, you will observe, cannot find a place in this system of classification: on the one hand, it falls short of universality; on the other hand, it is neither a regional nor a functional organisation. All the same, I believe that it has something to tell us about the present position and future prospects of international society, provided we do not confine ourselves to the method of external observation and classification. I feel that it is time for me to get into the wood.

You can imagine me in the tangle of trees and undergrowth, casting about for the Commonwealth path. All at once I come upon a familiar signpost. It is a speech which Smuts made as the guest of both Houses of Parliament on the evening of 15 May 1917, the speech which put the word Commonwealth into public circulation as a new name for the British Empire. Let me recall the circumstances. Lloyd George had come into power at the end of 1916, and one of his first acts had been to call an Imperial War Cabinet or Imperial War Conference (actually, two series of meetings were held in parallel under these two names) in order to discuss and decide upon war measures and peace aims. Despite the protests of the South Africans, a third large subject was put upon the agenda—nothing less than the constitution of the British Empire. At this time the Round Table groups, which Milner's young men (as they had once been) had established throughout the Empire, were at the peak of their influence. They believed that the time was ripe—now or never—to win acceptance for their great cause, Imperial Federation. Some of them, Lionel Curtis in particular, believed that this was the only way of turning the Empire into a Commonwealth and thereby ensuring its survival.

Smuts was determined to kill this scheme once and for all. It was he who drafted the resolution which, as one of his South African colleagues inelegantly expressed it, 'put the lid on Lionel Curtis and Co.'. This did not mean that Smuts was hostile to the Commonwealth; it meant merely that he had his own conception of its meaning and destiny—not the federalistic superstate which Lionel Curtis believed in, but an association of free nations living and working together within the circle of the Crown. As for the name: it had been familiar to Smuts and to his friend Merriman (a great and nowadays too much forgotten South African) for ten years or more. Smuts felt that 'Curtis and Co.' had misappropriated this shining name. The time had come for him to take it back again and put it to its proper use.

On the evening of 15 May 1917, he began his speech by discussing the war situation. The Germans (he said in effect) seem to think that they are winning the war but they are wrong. They may have been winning the victories but we shall win the war. From the four corners of the world we are gathering our strength. *We*—but who are *we*? He answered his rhetorical questions with a shattering paradox. We are not an empire, he declared. We are not British.

I think that we are inclined to make mistakes in thinking about this group of nations to which we belong because too often we think about it as one State. We are not a State. The British Empire is much more than a State. I think the very expression 'Empire' is misleading, because it makes people think that we are one community, to which the word Empire can appropriately be applied. Germany is an Empire. Rome was an Empire. India is an Empire. But we are a system of nations. We are not a State, but a community of states and nations. We are far greater than any empire which has ever existed, and by using this ancient expression we really disguise the main fact that our whole position is different, and that we are not one state or nation or empire, but a whole world by ourselves, consisting of many nations, of many states, and all sorts of communities, under one flag. . . . We are a system of states, and not a stationary but a dynamic and evolving system, always going forward to new destinies.

If we are not an empire, he went on, why call ourselves one? If we are something new, we had better give ourselves a new name. Let us take the name of Commonwealth.

Smuts believed the Commonwealth to have its roots deep down in the soil of British freedom. When one looked at it in the context of legal and constitutional history, it was British and would remain so. But it was no longer British when one looked at it in the context of cultural and national history.

All the empires we have known in the past and that exist today are founded on the idea of assimilation, of trying to force human material into one mould. Your whole idea and basis is entirely different. You do not want to standardise the nations of the British Empire; you want to develop them towards fuller, greater nationality. . . . That is the fundamental fact we have to bear in mind—that the British Commonwealth of Nations does not stand for standardisation or denationalisation, but for the fuller, richer and more various life of all the nations comprised in it.

Even the nations which have fought against it, like my own, must feel that their interests, their language, their religion, are as safe and secure under the British flag as those of your own household and your own blood.

There, in a few vivid strokes, we have it—the picture of the Commonwealth as we see it today, a polity of many sovereignties and many cultures. But how in the world can such a polity be held together? Smuts put this question to himself and gave a confident answer. There were three things, he said, which would hold the Commonwealth together: common loyalty to the Crown; the technique of conference; common values. To the champions of Imperial Federation these must have seemed flimsy links; but Smuts believed them strong enough to ensure unity in diversity and maintain the Commonwealth as a Great Power—'far greater', he declared, 'than any empire which has ever existed'.

To what extent this confidence was to be justified by the events of the next two generations we must soon inquire; but first let us follow Smuts on his missionary journeys to spread the gospel of the Commonwealth amongst the Gentiles. At the end of 1917 he set out for Switzerland to hold secret talks with Count Mensdorf, formerly Austrian Ambassador in London and now commissioned by his imperial master to sound out the possibilities of peace. Smuts tried to convince Mensdorf that there was still time for the Hapsburg Empire to save itself by decentralising itself on the grand scale, by recognising the autonomy and equality of its constituent nationalities —in short, by transforming itself into a Commonwealth. Mensdorf felt the thrill of this splendid vision; but he knew in his heart that it would never be realised; the weight of the German alliance and of its own past lay too heavy upon the Hapsburg Empire. Smuts was compelled in the following nine months to admit this as a fact; but he still believed that it need not have been a fact if only the Hapsburgs had been able to recognise the potentialities contained in their history.[1] A year after his talk with Mensdorf, he set down in a few sentences his own interpretation of the historical significance of empires.

Nations in their march to power tend to pass the purely national bounds; hence arise the empires which embrace various nations, sometimes related in blood and institutions, sometimes again different in race and hostile in temperament. In a rudimentary way all such composite empires of the past were leagues of nations, keeping the peace among the constituent nations but unfortunately doing so not on the basis of freedom but of repression. Usually one dominant nation in the group overcame, coerced and kept the rest under. The principle of nationality became overstrained and over-developed, and nourished itself by exploiting other weaker nationalities. Nationality overgrown became imperialism, and the empire led a troubled existence on the ruin of the freedom of its constituent parts. That was the evil of the system; but with however much friction and oppression, the peace was usually kept among the nations falling within the empire. The empires have all broken down, and today the British Commonwealth of Nations remains the only embryo league of nations because it is based on the principle of national freedom and political decentralisation.[2]

These sentences represent historical generalisation on

---

[1] Smuts no doubt underestimated the strength of the centrifugal forces, which was due to the fact that most of the nations straddled the boundaries of the Hapsburg Empire and could not achieve complete political unity unless those boundaries were rubbed out.

[2] *The League of Nations. A Practical Suggestion.* Printed in David Hunter Miller, *The Drafting of a Covenant*, New York and London, 1928, vol. II, p. 25.

the heroic scale. From the firm ground of his experience of the Commonwealth, Smuts had taken a leap into universal history. We may say, if we like, that his leap was an holistic one, provided we first make sure that we understand what he meant by whole-making. It had no necessary connection with mere size. In his sociology, as in his cosmology, Smuts laid stress upon the inward, rather than the outward character of the evolutionary, whole-building process. The highest achievement of this process so far was the evolution of the human person, who is not at all conspicuous among natural objects by his mere physical dimensions. Similarly, in the political universe, the nation is less conspicuous in its physical dimensions than the empire; all the same, it is more of an individual, a more highly developed whole.

National individuality, national self-determination, was the first article of Smuts's political faith. This meant, in practical application, that empires—the British Empire no less than all the others—had to be broken up. But something was needed to take their place. A nation outside society, like a man outside the State, must be either a beast or a god. If the self-determination of nations was the first article of Smuts's political faith, the sociability of nations was the second article. This sociability, if it were to be real, must express itself in institutions. Smuts believed that traditional institutions saved a great deal of trouble. He thought the nations of the Commonwealth extremely lucky in being free to develop their own destinies under the aegis of the British Crown. He thought the Danubian nations extremely unlucky in having to start building all over again on the rubble of the Hapsburg monarchy. He doubted whether they would ever build successfully unless the League of Nations gave them a helping hand. But what roots in tradition would the League have? Smuts was writing a programme for it before it was made. He knew that it could not possibly escape from being a fabricated institution. Then let it be fabricated, he argued, on the model of the British Commonwealth.

And from this point of view let us proceed at once to discard the idea of a super-state which is in the minds of some people. No new super-sovereign is wanted in the new world that is now arising. . . . The old empires were ruined by their theories of sovereignty, which meant centralisation, absorption, and denationalisation of the weaker national constituents of the population. The great league of nations, like the lesser league already existing in the British Empire, will have to avoid the old legal concepts of imperialism in the new world of freedom. We shall likewise have to abandon all ideas of federation or confederation as inapplicable to the case, and not likely to be agreed to by any of the existing sovereign states. We are inevitably driven to the conference system now in vogue in the constitutional practice of the British Empire, although it will necessarily have to be applied with very considerable modifications to the complex world conditions obtaining under the league.[1]

The Commonwealth path along which Smuts has been guiding me has now joined the League of Nations path. I can see that I had better get out of the wood before I get entangled in the undergrowth of international politics. When I stand at a distance from the wood and try to make out its general shape I can see two intermingling projects of CIVITAS MAXIMA, the Commonwealth and the League. In the years between the wars their essential

[1] *Op. cit.*, p. 38.

similarity became more easily recognisable as the old façade of imperial sovereignty was torn away from the Commonwealth structure. After the Statute of Westminster, the Commonwealth was just as clearly a *société des nations* (though of course a smaller and less imposing one) as the League itself. In both societies, the legislative and executive functions belonged to the constituent nations, not to a central authority. The Imperial Conference, like the Council and Assembly of the League, was essentially a diplomatic gathering.

How then are we to explain the fact that the League collapsed while the Commonwealth survived? Attempts were made at the time and have been made since to find an explanation in constitutional terms. It has been suggested that America might have come into the League if the obligations of membership had not been so strictly defined; on the other hand, it has been suggested that they should have been more strictly defined to prevent powerful and egotistical nations from slipping through the gaps in the Covenant. Both suggestions seem excessively legalistic and oblivious of the political realities. For example, the political isolation which kept America out of the League would almost certainly have operated in some other way even if she had entered it: at any rate, it is very difficult to imagine America leading or even following a hue and cry against the Japanese in Manchuria, the Italians in Abyssinia or the Germans in the Rhineland and Central Europe. Yet these were the three crises which exposed the facts of power that destroyed the League. Power belonged to the sovereign state; League or no League, a strong and determined state would take what it wanted unless or until a combination of the other sovereign states mobilised their joint power in support of the League to restrain it. The League collapsed through lack of a common will.

Attempts have also been made to explain in constitutional terms the vitality of the Commonwealth. For example, a great deal was heard between the wars of the *inter se* doctrine of Commonwealth relations, according to which resort could not be had to international law for the determination of the extent of the obligations existing between parts of the Commonwealth. Implied in this doctrine was the assertion that the Commonwealth was not fully an international society but that differences between its members were in some way or other a 'domestic' matter. Mr J. E. S. Fawcett, who has written the clearest account of the *inter se* doctrine, is willing to admit that it may have served some purpose during the 1920's in smoothing the transition from a unitary empire, in which there was devolution of power, to an association of independent states with full international status; but he doubts whether the doctrine counted for anything, except perhaps in commercial treaties, after 1930.[1] Certainly, it was by their own political decision that the sovereign and independent countries of the Commonwealth went to war in 1939. Their decision—always excepting Eire, which by her own sovereign decision kept out of the war —can be explained by the triple link which Smuts had emphasised in his speech on 15 May 1917—loyalty to the Crown, the technique of conference, common values.

[1] J. E. S. Fawcett, *The* Inter Se *Doctrine of Commonwealth Relations*, Commonwealth Papers No. 5, London, 1958.

But is this explanation sufficient? There was another factor, which we may call British hegemony. The old Empire was not yet finished, the new Commonwealth was not yet complete: a cynic might say that Great Britain, for the last time in her history, was getting the best of both worlds.

Let us now move forward a generation and compare the Commonwealth of 1960 with the one whose advent Smuts acclaimed in 1917 and whose existence he fought for in 1939 and the following six years of bitter conflict. The prophesies of 1917 have been fulfilled and more than fulfilled under the head of nationality; but under the head of sociability there is a more complicated story to tell. *British Empire* has become in our day a name of the vanished past, completely out of fashion except, perhaps, among my fellow countrymen, who seem to have a genius for being progressive and old fashioned at the same time. *British Commonwealth* is going rapidly out of fashion; most people prefer the noun without the adjective. These changes of nomenclature reflect changes in the political realities more sweeping than those that Smuts foresaw in 1917. Some dozen sovereign states enjoy today full membership of the Commonwealth, and in the combined total of their citizens people of British stock would barely amount to one-quarter. The constitutions of Commonwealth states are about half-and-half monarchical and republican and the tide of republicanism seems still to be rising. To be sure, the Queen remains Head of the Commonwealth; but 'the Queen's men'— I am quoting a phrase of my Prime Minister, Mr R. G. Menzies—are a diminishing proportion of Commonwealth citizens. Moreover, the Crown which some of us retain in our constitutions is no longer an indivisible Crown. However we look at it, there has been a striking diminution of the symbolic and procedural unity of monarchy which Smuts acclaimed as the first bond of the Commonwealth. His third bond, community of values, has also suffered some painful diminutions. Democratic, or at least constitutional government used to be, but is no longer, regarded as an essential qualification for Commonwealth membership. It used to be said that war between Commonwealth members was unthinkable; but today we can think only too easily of war between South Africa and other Commonwealth states in Africa[1] or between South Africa and India. And for a decade or more we have seen India and Pakistan arming themselves against each other.

What kind of a community, then, is the Commonwealth of these days, if indeed it remains a community? In the eyes of some people it has become a joke—a bitter joke or a merry joke, according to temperament.[2] One thing at least is plain to everybody: the Commonwealth remains no longer, as Smuts believed in 1917 that it was destined to remain, 'more powerful than any empire that has ever existed'. If it were to qualify as a Great Power, two things would be requested: first, a sufficiency of resources; secondly, a willingness to pool those resources in 'the common cause'. At present, neither of these conditions is satisfied. To be sure, when we take stock of present

[1] This was written before the decision of May 1961 leading to South Africa's withdrawal from the Commonwealth.

[2] See the Parkinsonian article, *Cwthmas*, in *The Economist*, 27 December 1958.

economic potentialities and past political performance, we cannot feel 100 per cent certain that they will never be satisfied in some future testing-time; but here and now the Commonwealth is not a competitor in the Great Power stakes.

A pessimist might say that the Commonwealth is merely a device for easing and sweetening the process of imperial disintegration, a stage along the road, not to CIVITAS MAXIMA, but to international anarchy. It may be so. But to me it seems just as realistic to envisage the nations of the Commonwealth, and of the whole world, engaged upon a painful and difficult climb out of the Hobbist pit and up the rocky path which leads to international order. The climb calls for certain capabilities in which the Commonwealth is a good training ground. For example, it calls for the capacity to combine order and liberty within the process of change: in this, the most difficult of the political arts, the Commonwealth has had a long practice; in our century particularly, change—more often than not peaceful change—has been its *métier*. Again, it calls for the damping down of fanaticism, for a spirit of patience and (in the old sense of the word) comprehension; we find this spirit expressed in Hooker's *Ecclesiastical Polity*, Halifax's *Character of a Trimmer* and much other writing of a distinct English flavour; we find it embodied in the legal and constitutional practice which still remains dominant, with whatever local variations, in the majority of Commonwealth countries. These virtues are essentially procedural. They find expression in those customs and institutions of mutual consultation and conference that Smuts considered vital for the survival of the

Commonwealth. Here at last, despite some spasms of carelessness and one calamitous lapse, we find a bond of unity which today is certainly more systematised, and on the whole more operative, than it was when Smuts expounded the significance of the Commonwealth that summer evening nearly half a century ago.

Let us agree to look upon the Commonwealth as an interesting segment of international society, not a *bloc*, but a group of sovereign nations whose members have developed to an unusual degree the habit of mutual consultation. Some of us may feel in our hearts that the roots of unity are deeper than this, but by taking the matter-of-fact view we shall avoid the risk of over-pitching our expectations. At the same time, we shall recognise the great responsibilities and opportunities which confront this matter-of-fact Commonwealth. It has a footing in most of the problem-areas of the world. Through one or other of its members, and sometimes a sizeable cluster of them, it shares the business of the Atlantic Community, the Afro-Asian Community, the Pacific Community—of all the oceans and all the continents except South America. Given the habit of consultation between its members, it can play at all times a useful, and sometimes a creative part in the world's political business.

The central clearing-house of the world's political business is the United Nations Organisation. I have not the knowledge to say anything original about this institution; but there are one or two elementary facts about it which deserve to be repeated and underlined. Like its predecessor, the League of Nations, it is not—at any rate, not yet—

the parliament and government of mankind, but an institution of international diplomacy. At San Francisco in 1945, when the United Nations were being made, extraordinary pains were taken to forget the Covenant and to acclaim the Charter as a completely new chapter in the book of human history. 'We, the Peoples of the United Nations'—these words were substituted, at the insistence of American idealism, for the opening words of the preamble which Smuts had drafted. They embalm an act of colossal self-deception. For it is not the Peoples, but the Sovereign States of the world who confront each other in the Council and General Assembly of the United Nations, just as they used to do in the Council and Assembly of the League of Nations.

Nevertheless, the winds of change are blowing. International organisations, like national constitutions and other human institutions, have a habit of growing and changing without consistent regard for what their 'founding fathers' have tried to lay down as being best for them. Consider, for example, the veto, which was the centre of fierce debate in 1945 at San Francisco. The Charter, as it emerged from this debate, enumerated by name five Powers as the possessors of this special privilege. Looked at in the large, the privilege amounted to this: that the named Powers would retain their ancient right of being judges in their own causes and, it may be added, in the causes of such lesser states as might be enrolled among their clients. An unfortunate error of draftsmanship, the simple-minded constitutionalist may say: but it can never be an error to recognise plain political fact. Had there been no veto, Soviet Russia would never have joined the United Nations Organisation. Nor would the United States have joined it. The veto was the basic condition upon which the United Nations came into existence. But can we say today that it remains the basic condition of their continuing existence? It has been blunted by over-use. Since the Uniting for Peace Resolution of 1950, it has been side-stepped on successive occasions by action of the General Assembly. The French did no good for themselves by using it in 1956 during the Suez crisis. During the Congo crisis of 1960, no attempt even was made to use it. Everything depended then, not upon the hopelessly divided Security Council, but upon the Secretary-General and the General Assembly.

The shift of interest and initiative from the Security Council to the General Assembly is a development of great significance. It has coincided in time with a vast redistribution of power among the nations of the world. The concept of a praesidium of five named Powers, each possessing the right of veto, was antique even at San Francisco; now it is dead. Today there are only two Great Powers in UNO. Perhaps even they are being left behind in the march of events. I can only guess (although I am sure that a pertinacious student of international politics could do much better) at the meaning of all these changes.

What, for example, are we to make of the sudden and vast increase in the membership of the United Nations? At the General Assembly of 1960 nearly one hundred states were represented. In virtue of their common feature of sovereignty, they all enjoyed equal voting rights, although some of them were puny in power. Cyprus (to mention but one of the new arrivals) had a population of less than half a million. On the other hand, Communist China, with a population of many hundreds of millions, was unrepresented. Students of history and politics are only too well aware of the dangers which beset national representative systems which fail to embody the real and effective forces which are operative in society. Is there not a warning here? And, apart from the special case of China, is not vigilance required to ensure that contradiction and discord do not arise between the representational development of the United Nations and its functional development?

A word may be said here about the Specialised Agencies, such as the World Health Organisation, which are performing important functions under the aegis of the General Assembly. One has the feeling, or at least the hope, that their work possesses increasing significance for individual human beings in many countries of the world. Perhaps they are blazing one of the important trails which lead towards human solidarity. Should this prove to be so, one would expect gains of extra-special significance from the International Atomic Energy Agency, which was established in 1956 to develop the new sources of energy for the prosperity and peace of mankind.

And yet, the sovereign states amongst which mankind is partitioned still face each other 'in posture of war': or, if that is to put the matter too pessimistically, in posture of deterrence. The giants among them have refused to surrender to world authority the powers of world-wide devastation which they hold in their hands. Indeed, it is to be doubted whether the world authority is yet in sight which would be competent to administer these powers.

UNO wears a double aspect: it is at one and the same time
CIVITAS MAXIMA struggling to be born and an arena of the
Cold War. In the danger zone through which humanity
is now passing the powers of life and death remain with
the separate sovereign states; in particular, with the mam-
moth states. The fate of mankind will depend for some
time yet upon the prudence of their governments.

I shall leave the last word with Smuts. Towards the
close of the Second World War, as he reflected upon the
prodigious advance of science and its application to war,
he found himself in uneasy balance between hope and
foreboding. Sometimes he thought that science would
do for humanity what statesmanship had failed to do. 'So
I am not without hope of the future,' he wrote in January
1945, 'even if that hope is based on despair—human nature
being at last *coerced* into proper behaviour, where no other
appeal would do.'

This was his first thought when news was flashed round
the world of the atomic bombs dropped upon Hiroshima
and Nagasaki. 'We are now forewarned of what is coming if war is not ended for good. . . . At last a discovery
has been made which should put war out of court for
good and all.' It seemed plain to him that the control of
sub-atomic energy had now become the paramount
international question and that something far more drastic
would have to be done than had recently been achieved
at San Francisco through the Charter of the United
Nations.

But very soon he began to doubt whether this something would be done. The sovereign states who were in

charge of the human family showed no sign of allowing themselves to be 'coerced' by science into good behaviour. 'Even the atomic bomb', he wrote in November 1945, 'may not be able to give us peace. It becomes a rivalry as to who can make the most dreadful and destructive bomb.' He believed that the new powers which man had achieved over nature called for a new disposition of the human head and heart; but could discover no sign that this mental and spiritual adaptation was taking place. 'It is power, science, economics, these three. But Paul's three—the real Big Three—I see little of. And yet without Hope, Faith and Love this fair world is lost.'

And yet he did not lose heart. For many years past, and particularly throughout the six years of war, he had concentrated all the energy that he could spare for study upon two widely separated areas of knowledge, the New Testament and pre-history. These studies confirmed the conviction that he had held throughout his life of the sovereignty in long term of good over evil, manifesting itself not least in the evolution of the universe and, within that evolution, in the ascent of man. From the many letters which he wrote upon this theme I shall choose two quotations, one contemporaneous with the Battle of Britain and the other with the aftermath of Hiroshima. In August 1940 he wrote to Mrs Gillett:

Our progress so far has not been contemptible. 10,000 years ago we had reached the neolithic stage. 20,000 years ago we were just trying to straighten ourselves in the Neanderthal form. In another 20,000 years we may almost reach the stature of the sons of God. Today we are with the Hitlers and the Mussolinis, but we should not despair.

In November 1945 he wrote to the Abbé Breuil, whom he had rescued from exile and poverty in Portugal during the war and set to work on the study of African cave paintings:

> Man is perhaps the youngest of the mammalia species, and yet what a progress we have made in the short span of our history and pre-history! When I compare the tools of the primitive sub-humans with the stage of achievement we have reached in, say, half a million years, I realise what an enormous future advance is still before us. . . . Three cheers for the human race!

He gave a still clearer indication of this line of thought twelve months later, when he took a day off from a distressful struggle at the United Nations to visit the Natural History Museum of New York in the company of three distinguished students of early man.

> I remarked that when I study History I am inclined sometimes to be a pessimist, but when I study Pre-history I become an optimist. . . . On the short time scale of history, you may doubt whether and in what respects we have advanced beyond Socrates and Plato and Athens, but when you see those awful gorilla forms of your far-off ancestry how could you doubt about the advances? And to speculate on what might be a million years hence!

Indeed, it is understandable that the sanguine and the sombre chords which are intermingled in the emotional dispositions of most of us should vibrate alternately in response to our alternating reflections upon the condition of man, as we picture it in different dimensions of time. On the one hand, it is so tempting to glorify our species when we look back upon its millennial struggle with brute creation, upon its Promethean victories over nature, culminating in these latter-day explorations of the atomic particles and of outer space: to glorify our species still more when we look forward to the unnumbered millennia ahead and envisage the indefinite prolongation of man's majestic ascent. On the other hand, it is just as tempting to curse the time in which we live, when the sovereign states which history has bequeathed to us play with the new powers as children play with toys and threaten to destroy, not merely each other, but *homo sapiens* himself and the world which he is making in his own image.

All the same, there are people who challenge this dichotomy between the long-term and the short-term views of the human situation. I read the other day a sardonic essay by Sir John Lomax, who presents pre-history and history as a single tragedy or farce of the human fate. According to Sir John, cerebration is both the glory and the doom of man; it makes him the monarch of all he surveys and at the same time condemns him to mass suicide. To his wonderful cortex he owes all his intellectual triumphs and all his moral aspirations; but his cortex is the slave of his thalamus, that engine of blind struggle, robbery and murder.[1]

Is this a serious biological hypothesis or is it literary fun? If the latter, I can enjoy it, just as I enjoy Swift's yahoos: if the former, I think the biologists and the psychologists had better set to work as a matter of urgency to test the hypothesis. We may as well know the worst. Not that we can do anything about it, if Sir John Lomax is right. But is he?

---

[1] *Twentieth Century*, October, 1960, 'Why We Like War'.

It would take a lot of proof to make me a biological determinist.

The last sentence was intended to close the chapter; but perhaps it is too cryptic. It is a way of saying that *homo sapiens* need not despair of his own rationality unless and until he gets proof to the contrary. By his genius for disciplined thought he has got himself into a difficult situation; he had better employ the same genius in getting himself out of it.

The burden of thought falls first upon governments. I have suggested that their sovereign virtue at the present time is prudence. It would be too much to expect from them the 'Hope, Faith and Love' whose absence Smuts deplored. These virtues ennoble the individual life and sweeten society; but we should not ask our political rulers (the Chancellor of the Exchequer, for example) to practise them immoderately. No: prudence will do well enough, combined with courage and (let us hope) at least some flicker of creative imagination.

Governments deserve more support than they are getting from academic people. Since my arrival in England (in July 1960) I have detected among my academic colleagues a reluctance, which reminds me too much of the mood of the 1930's, to think rigorously about the problems discussed in Chapter I. They are left usually to the specialists of strategical study, who in their turn tend to brush aside the problems discussed in Chapters II, III and IV. There seems to be an urgent need for academic study in breadth and depth of *all* the interrelated problems of war and peace.

These problems, of course, are far more extensive, complicated and various than has been suggested in the present course of chapters. A reconnaissance in strength would need to have not four, but twenty prongs.

COSTS OF THE COLD WAR

In chapter I, I suggested that a powerful industrial state would be able at need to devote to defence a much larger proportion of its national income (GNP) than has generally been admitted in public discussion. I also suggested that the competition for power between the United States and Soviet Russia, under present circumstances, has a tendency to make the plateau of defence expenditure upward-tilting.

I made these suggestions with some qualms, because nowadays I do not read the periodicals in which such matters are currently discussed but depend upon the books which from time to time come my way. When I was preparing the lecture on which Chapter I was based, the most recent book on this subject which I had seen was *Mobilising Economic Resources for War* by T. Scitovsky, E. Shaw and L. Tarshis (The *RAND* Corporation and McGraw-Hill Book Company, New York, 1951). The authors, writing in the shadow of the Korean War, offered a blueprint for American economic mobilisation which assumed some cutting back of civilian living standards but still permitted strong capital formation and at the same time provided for the war machine, at the peak of effort, 57.86 per cent of Gross National Product. These estimates are relevant to my argument in so far as they show that the American economy is capable of making a far greater contribution to national strategy than it made during the last war; but it is irrelevant inasmuch as it still envisages the defence effort as a series of valleys and peaks, rather than 'the monotonous, dismal prolongation of a plateau'.

A day or two before I delivered my lecture at Belfast, news came to me of the publication of *The Economics of Defense in the Nuclear Age*, by Charles J. Hitch and Roland N. McKean (The *RAND* Corporation and Harvard University Press, 1960). I thought that I might find, after reading this book, that I should have to alter the last part of my lecture; but it has not proved necessary. The authors, of course, write with far greater economic sophistication and knowledge than I possess; but they take great pains to make two identical points which I have made, namely:

(1) The valley-and-peak image of a defence effort has been superseded by the plateau image.

E.G.

'In an all-out thermonuclear war the superior economic war potential of the United States is important only to the extent that it has been diverted to security purposes before war starts.' (p. 15)

'Economic strength that is used for national security purposes in time is the embodiment of military power.' (p. 16)

(2) The force of competition will tend to give the plateau a persistent upward tilt. This argument is developed at length in Chapter VI, where stress is laid upon the advantages which U.S.S.R. possesses over U.S.A. in promoting the rapid growth of industry and in ensuring high expenditure on defence. The authors believe that Russian expenditure on defence in 1955, which is shown in a table on page 95 as 13 per cent of GNP, in comparison with America's 10 per cent, is in fact very much higher (15 to 20 per cent) when reckoned in terms of dollars. They expect that the Russians will continue to push this percentage upwards, and write (page 97):

It would take a highly defense-minded populace in the United States to support a military budget that persistently amounted to 15 per cent of GNP. The Soviet Union faces less severe political constraints, and may easily, as the economy grows, devote 20 to 25 per cent of GNP to defense.... If the Soviet Union should devote 25 per cent of GNP to military purposes, the populace of the United States might well become 'highly defense-minded' and put more than 15 per cent of United States resources to the same purpose.

They do not ask the question, 'How much more?'

The authors differ only in one respect from the argument put forward in Chapter I: namely, in their unwillingness to consider the possibility that the above-mentioned competition with Russia in defence preparations might push the United States in the direction of a controlled economy.

Perhaps I should say again, in case the point was missed, that Chapter I contains no recommendations; readers of Swift will not mistake the intent of my 'modest proposal' about duckweed. Nor does the chapter contain any predictions. One can envisage circumstances, pleasant or unpleasant, in which the Cold War, with

Appendix I

its hopes, fears and costs, might cease to dominate international politics. Even within the context of the Cold War, one can envisage the possibility of technological and strategical changes which, in combination with continuing economic growth, might give the plateau of defence expenditure a downward tilt. But at present its tilt seems to be upwards. The chapter suggests some reasons for this and some possible consequences, *if* this trend is not reversed.

SOME REFLECTIONS ON CHAPTER IV

By J. E. S. Fawcett

THE questions whether international law is binding, or in what sense it can be called law at all, are not of course to be evaded. But it is perhaps impossible at the present time to give a wholly satisfactory answer to them. However, though I am closer to the 'sombre school' temperamentally than to their opposites, I would want to put the case of international law somewhere between them; for there seems to me to be encouragement in the fact that a more satisfactory answer to these questions may be given in 1960 than could have been given in 1910.

To see what is involved in this whole matter of the status and function of international law, it is helpful to set down first the kind of questions which lawyers and politicians and 'the man on the top of the Clapham omnibus' variously ask about it: Are the rules of international law obligatory? Is international law law? Does it govern anything but minor patterns of international relations? How is it to be enforced? Need we observe its rules when it is not in our interest to do so? Can international law prevent war? Would world law bring world peace? If strong nations can break international-law rules at will, what is the use of it?

So the lawyer contrasts the enforceability of international law unfavourably with that of his more familiar national law and concludes that international law is not law at all; the politician is tempted to adapt this conclusion to practice and to waive the rules when he thinks he can get away with it; and the man on the bus is left in confusion, impatient with planners of early world government but nevertheless frustrated in certain deep-rooted social instincts.

We see then in these typical approaches two great issues, one legal, the other political: first, are the rules of international law 'obligating'? Second, if so, can these rules help to spread peace and order in the world? What follows in this short space are no more than prolegomena to answers to these questions.

Appendix II (J. E. S. Fawcett)

(1) The first question cannot of course be answered by definitions. Austin transformed international law into a kind of international morality by defining law in a way which excluded it. A definition of law could equally be constructed, which not only embraced international law but even gave it primacy amongst legal orders. But neither course leads anywhere.

(2) The tacit comparison of international law with municipal law by reference to a standard of enforceability, a comparison which often underlies disenchantment with international law and the denial of the title 'law' to the regularities of international relations, is, I think, misconceived for three reasons:

(a) In no legal order are there rules which are never broken, and there are many more honoured in the breach than in the observance. Instances could be found in many countries in such diverse fields of law and legislation as taxation, prostitution, divorce, customs evasion, anti-trust, gambling, or labour, where law enforcement varies from being weak to non-existent. Further, there are a dozen constitutions where provisions guaranteeing civil liberties are seldom enforced and are often in practice unenforceable: *corruptissima republica, plurimae leges*, said Tacitus. To say that the laws in these cases are nevertheless enforceable in principle and that this fact saves their character as law is to fall back on definition, and a definition in the tradition of Austin, which is strong against the acceptance as law of what has not been commanded by some father-figure in the form of a sovereign, or precedent-creating judge, or a sovereign or omnicompetent Parliament.

On the other side of the picture, international law is observed and applied more extensively and more consistently, in large things as well as small, than many of its critics seem to have noticed. It has admittedly been broken, and broken seriously, but, though the incidence of crime in a country may be an indicator of the state of its social health, the commission of serious crimes does not in itself imply that the society is mortally sick; and so international relations today are no more simply power politics and war than social life is simply crime and a drive for success and power.

(b) The comparison we are considering between international law and municipal law ignores the fact that sovereignty is an outmoded fiction. The apostles of sovereignty have seldom stood back and

127

looked at the State in its international setting. They have constructed an absolute sovereignty out of feudal notions of superior lordship, which is easy to accept as the expression of the internal highest power and authority of the State, that is to say, of the State seen in isolation; but absolute sovereignty in a community of states is meaningless: for here the continued political existence of each State depends both in fact and in theory on limitations upon the power and authority of every other. International law is the summary of these limitations. Its rules are not yet either wholly generalised or wholly articulate, but their suspension would even now spell the destruction of states.

(*c*) With the personalisation of the State an artificial distinction is made between international law, conceived as governing the State as international person, and municipal law which governs its internal working. Here we only too easily overlook the fact that the State, whatever its metaphysical structure, can act only through human agents, men and women, who by a complex process of delegation exercise the combined powers of their fellow-members in the community. It is they, appointed and acting under municipal law, who observe and enforce the rules of international law or abuse the power of the State to break them. The problem of enforceability lies here and not in the metaphysics of State sovereignty and personality where the search for obligation ends only in contradictions: for the enforcement of rules of law, whether municipal or international, rests upon their acceptance by the governed: if that acceptance is withheld or suppressed, law breaks down. So where the power and authority of the State is placed behind exclusive interests, be they political or economic, municipal law will no longer protect those excluded, and international order will be put in danger. The remarks in the lecture upon the subjectivity of governments, that *jus* and *societas* stand or fall together, and that at least in this century the disjunctive forces in international life are stronger than the conjunctive, are I think part of the same line of thinking, though there may be room for different views of the political facts.

We are now in a little better position to attempt an answer to the second main question: Can the rules of international law help to spread peace and order in the world?

(1) Law cannot create order, it is a product of order; but it can

rationalise, organise and extend it. What was once known as the 'publick Law of Europe' has taken root all over the world, growing together with local branches of international law as in India, for example, and Latin America. But the process is slow and it is idle to suppose that it will or can create World Government.

Here too the historical approach to international law can be misleading: the great breakdowns of international order (the two world wars, Manchuria, Abyssinia, Hungary) are pointed to as demonstrable failures of international law, but it seems as unreasonable to attribute, for example, the collapse of the League causally to some inherent defect in international law as to attribute Hitler's rise to power and abuse of it to some vice in the very highly developed municipal law of Germany.

(2) The main problem of international order is the isolation of force. Every community must, if it is to survive, succeed in bringing the use of force into few hands, controlled by the community: and so the world community has both to outlaw aggressive war and breaches of the peace and also to create the force to extinguish them if they occur. International law can positively help here not only as a 'civilising idea' but as a ready source of the forms of order without which no organisation is possible. Some progress has been made in the last twenty years, but it is slow, and the forces of conflict and death have a long start.